TRUTH & TRUST

THE FIRST TWO VICTIMS OF DOWNSIZING

Frank J. Navran

ATHABASCA UNIVERSITY EDUCATIONAL ENTERPRISES

Credits

TRUTH & TRUST
THE FIRST TWO VICTIMS OF DOWNSIZING

Material from *Executive Excellence* reprinted with permission from Executive Excellence; phone (801) 375-4060.

For information address Athabasca University Educational Enterprises, Athabasca University, Box 10,000, Athabasca, Alberta, Canada T9S 1A1.

Designed by Mark David Dunsire, Athabasca University

Canadian Cataloguing in Publication Data

Navran, Frank J., 1943-

Truth and trust: the first two victims of downsizing

Includes bibliographical references and index.

ISBN 0-919737-14-5

1. Downsizing of organizations. I. Title.

HD58.8.N39 1995 658.4 02 C95-900028-3

Contents

FRANK J. NAVRAN

Frank J. Navran, a manager, trainer and consultant for over 25 years, came to know about downsizing from three perspectives: survivor, victim and change agent. Frank has kept his job while others around him were losing theirs. He has seen his job reorganized out from under him. He has reengineered, restructured and redesigned client organizations resulting in others losing their jobs. Downsizing, no matter the point of view, was always more painful, more complex, and much more difficult to do right than most people expected.

Now as president of Navran Associates, an Atlanta-based training and consulting company, Frank is helping his client organizations deal with the subtleties and complexities of difficult business issues like downsizing, with a focus on how they impact organizational ethics, employment practices and service quality.

Acknowledgements

This book is a collective effort and as the named author I would be remiss if I failed to recognize those who provided support and assistance during the months preceding publication.

My sincere thanks to Jerry Brown who provided a wealth of domestic and international examples illustrative of the downsizing experience. Jerry also authored the "summary maps" at the end of each chapter and served admirably as both proofreader and sounding board as the chapters rolled out.

Thanks also to Maxim Jean-Louis and Kerry Joyes who shared the vision of *Truth and Trust* and whose support led Athabasca University Educational Enterprises to publish both the book and the video seminars that accompany it.

Finally to my family, Barbara, Lianne and Ian, who gave of their time and energy to make certain that I had the time and energy needed to create this book and whose love and support sustained me when the days got long and the deadlines grew nearer.

Thank you all. I hope this work is worthy of you.

Frank J. Navran
January 1995
Atlanta, Georgia

Preface

The challenge facing all organizations, public, private, for-profit, nonprofit, is the same: viability.

Organizations come into being to serve a purpose, to satisfy a want or need. They continue to exist for as long as they are believed to serve that purpose by a sufficient number of their customers. That is the essential truth for retail stores, manufacturers, government agencies, regulated utilities, professionals, artists and authors.

For most groups viability means maintaining a place in the market, serving some share of those who want or need what that organization provides. For some, such as governments and other natural monopolies, that share may near 100 percent. For others a fraction of a percent of the total market is a gracious plenty. However, when funding decreases, when profits shrink, when costs rise, whenever financial viability is threatened the organization must face tough decisions.

Usually that decision follows two paths. The organization seeks ways to maintain or increase income while simultaneously looking for ways to decrease operating costs.

Income is increased by growth. Market share is expanded for existing products and services, and new products and services are introduced to existing markets.

Concurrently, efficiencies are sought. Costs are controlled through a variety of tactics: hiring freezes, reduced capital investment, postponement of planned expansions. One of the strategies for cutting costs is to reduce the fixed expenses associated with employee salary/wages and benefits. It is done through restructuring, re-engineering, rightsizing, realignment, consolidation, centralization, decentralization, attrition and layoffs. We call that downsizing.

We cannot escape the reality of organizational downsizing. The daily headlines scream about major corporations laying off thousands of employees. No sooner has the shock of the first layoff worn off then they announce "further cuts". Governments have learned the lesson and they too are downsizing with alarming regularity.

This is a phenomenon which is defining the last two decades of the twentieth century. Those large, mature, stable institutions which promised their employees security, safety and lifetime employment are changing. There is no promise of job security anymore. Susan Barciela, writing for the Knight-Ridder newspaper syndicate, captured it eloquently when she said, "All of you out there in career land, repeat after me. Long term doesn't exist anymore."

In this book we will be exploring downsizing in its most popular forms. We will discover that all these strategies are responses to a common set of motives, based on a set of beliefs, half truth and half myth. We will discuss who makes the decision to downsize, and how they announce and implement the decision. Then, a look at how organizations deal with those who have been encouraged or required to leave.

The heart of this book deals with the survivors, those who remain in the organization after the downsizing initiative has been fully implemented. There are a common set of issues they face and by understanding those issues we discover the key to future success. Downsizing itself is not the organizational savior it is made out to be. The secret to success is in recognizing and responding to the organizational and individual needs that arise in the aftermath of the decision to reduce headcount. By understanding the issues and the changes implicit in them we can learn how to make downsizing fulfill its promise.

As the book wraps up we will look at the issue of responsibility, who is responsible for doing what, and then look to the future. This book ends on a positive note suggesting that the painful process of downsizing may be one of passage from stagnation and stagflation to a renewal of the American Dream for future generations.

We do not argue that this complex organizational decision is *by definition* morally wrong, evil or unfair. We will argue that it is poorly understood, insufficiently researched and rarely as effective in delivering on its promises as today's decision makers would hope.

As a consequence, downsizing often produces unforeseen consequences and creates unintended victims. We will name those victims in the belief that in so doing tomorrow's decision makers will be better prepared.

First among the unintended victims of downsizing are truth and trust. When the decision to downsize is made it is often accompanied by the decision to manage information flow and access, such that key organizational stakeholders are left with a mix of partial truths, speculations, misunderstandings and conjectures. The natural consequence of insufficient information is a disbelief in the validity of the decision to downsize and a distrust of those who made it.

Our ultimate message is that when truth and trust are sacrificed, downsizing fails. When they are preserved, downsizing works. This is a "how-to" book. The message is that there is a better way to implement this most difficult strategic decision, one which preserves truth and trust.

Chapter 1

The Downsizing Phenomenon

Why downsize? That question has occurred to millions who face the uncertainty of the rumor or announcement that their job might be the next one eliminated. The standard answers spring from tired, worn out phrases that have become organizational clichés: stay competitive, get lean and mean, do more with less. The suspicion lingers for those whose jobs are on the line that there must be a better way. This is a mistake. We never should have gotten in this situation in the first place. Somebody, somewhere, must have seen this coming and should have, could have, prevented it.

In most organizations the decision to downsize springs from a mixture of external influences and internally accepted promises and myths. It is only one of a number of alternative strategies being implemented, concurrently, to deal with a series of compelling forces that are wrenching the organization out of its complacency and into traumatic change.

The forces

Russell Ackoff, in a brilliant and insightful presentation to the AT&T management team, *circa* 1980, described the differences and limitations inherent in analytical thinking versus systemic thinking. *Analysis*, which Ackoff said has become synonymous with *thinking* in our culture, is the outgrowth of our belief that we can understand how things work by taking them apart. We remove the part, disassemble it and see how it works.

Systems thinking, what some call *synthesis,* suggests that some aspects of how things work are better understood by examining individual items or entities in relationship to their environment, that we understand better by learning how a system's components are interconnected. Part of understanding how things work comes from seeing how they fit together.

Systems thinking has revolutionized our understanding of organizations and why they succeed and fail. Organizations are classic systems. They meet the two criteria of a system: they are composed of interconnected subsystems and are, themselves, part of a larger "containing" system (what in organizational jargon is called a "supersystem"). By definition, every element of an organization's containing system is interconnected with the organization. Those external, interconnected systems are the external forces that shape the opportunities and constraints the organization faces.

Understand these external forces and you begin to understand why organizations act as they do. More importantly you can understand what organizations need to do if they are to survive and prosper.

David Nadler, in his Organization Performance Model (OPM), delineated some of the most essential external forces which drive organizational decision making. When these drives are understood and monitored, the organization responds to their demands proactively, seeing an emerging force and anticipating the moves necessary to take full advantage of inherent opportunities and to minimize the negative impact of inherent constraints. When organizations fail to attend to these external forces, they are forced to respond reactively. The resulting knee-jerk decisions are preordained by external forces and severely limit the organization's options.

What are these forces? Nadler defines several that may drive the decision to downsize:

- customers
- competitors
- vendors/suppliers
- shareholders/constituents
- political entities/politicians
- regulators
- technology

- domestic and foreign economic conditions
- unions and the labor pool

Whether the decision is reactive or proactive it is as much a matter of timing as any other variable. If the impact on the organization is anticipated the response, the mid-course correction, can be proactive, with a wider range of available options. If the organization ignores and/or denies the impact of external forces it will be boxed in with few, if any, options for survival. The worst case is when the organization puts off responding too long and fails altogether.

Downsizing has become a global trend as well. While 87 per cent of domestic organizations undertook cost-cutting initiatives during the last five years, 86 per-cent of companies abroad also downsized. U.S., Canada, United Kingdom, Germany, and Japan have all increased downsizing initiatives drastically during the last six years.

Lisa Baggerman,
Industry Week,
1/18/93

Let's look briefly at each of these external forces and see how they individually or in combination could motivate the decision to downsize.

Customers

There is an old adage in business: nothing happens until someone buys something. Theodore Levitt, Harvard Business School professor and renowned strategist, is credited with the observation that the ultimate purpose of every organization is to attract and retain customers.

Every organization has customers. Simply defined, customers are those who use what the organization produces. That product can be a tangible object, information, intellectual property, policy or whatever. Other definitions suggest that the customer is the one who pays for the product, not necessarily the one who uses it. Whatever definition you choose, the reality remains that customers determine your success through their ongoing demand for what you do. If nobody wants or needs what you produce, you lose. Without demand, there is no need for supply, and that's true for buggy whips, widgets or governments.

Customers are changing. They are better educated, better informed and better organized. Their expectations regarding product quality, service quality, ease of doing business and responsiveness are rising. They want more, better, faster and cheaper and if you do not give it to them they will take their business elsewhere.

Even in monopolies and government service, customers are more insistent on value, getting a fair return for their investment. As a consequence, organizations are having to find ways to deliver more, better, faster and cheaper. More suggests improved productivity and complexity, more product and more features. Better suggests fewer defects, increased reliability and ease of use. Faster means shorter delivery intervals, faster maintenance and repair. Cheaper is obvious. Even if the total price goes up, the price per unit of performance or value must go down.

Computers are the archtypical model of more, better, faster and cheaper. Compare shopping for a PC today with ten years ago.

One thousand 1985 U.S. dollars could buy a computer with:

- a 10-inch monochrome monitor
- up to 1/2 megabyte of random access memory (RAM)
- up to 20 megabytes of hard disk storage
- an operating speed of about eight megahertz

Even if the techno-babble is meaningless to you, just look at today's numbers. One thousand 1995 U.S. dollars (which have a real value significantly less than in 1985) can buy:

- a 33 to 50 megahertz computer
- a 14-inch high-resolution, color monitor
- four or more megabytes of RAM
- 200+ megabytes of hard disk storage

Today's computer even comes fully loaded with software, which if bought independently, would cost more than the computer itself. As an added attraction this computer is MS-DOS and Windows capable. Finally, if you are a careful shopper, you can get it equipped for CD-ROM, the latest "must" for every computer.

Apply that same magnitude of improvement in the price:value ratio to the automobile and you could buy a Rolls Royce for $5,000 that would carry six in comfort at speeds up to 200 mph, fully equipped with the latest in safety and comfort features and get 60 to 70 miles per gallon.

Customers place demands on organizations because of their rising expectations. Their demands for more, better, faster and cheaper require that the organization respond by desperately seeking ways to deliver what the customer wants. One of the strategies for meeting that demand is downsizing.

Competitors

Where do customers get the crazy idea that they are entitled to more, better, faster and cheaper or that it is even available? From your competitors. That is the basis for any competitive advantage. Giving the customer more for less does two things: it attracts customers and it raises their expectations.

Expectations are the natural consequence of experience. Once you experience improved service, for example, you come to value it and then expect it. Competition today is a never-ending game of expectation leap frog. The driver for organizations is to *exceed* customers' expectations to gain the short-term advantage over the competitor who set those expectations in the first place. Long term, recognize that your most competent competitors will find ways to out do you, starting the competitive cycle all over again.

The only apparent solution is to consort with competitors to limit what each will offer/deliver to customers, to agree on pricing strategies and to limit choices. We have a name for that practice. We call it *anti-trust violation*, and it will land you in jail and close your organization's doors forever.

Competitive pressure is a reality. It won't go away. It also motivates the organization to find ways to drive costs down. The biggest fixed cost in many organizations is people-related. Fewer people equates with lower operating costs. If the job can be done with fewer people, the argument in favor of downsizing is compelling.

Slow growth in gross domestic product (GDP) during the year accompanied the second consecutive annual drop in jobs and hours worked. The discrepancy between rising GDP and lower employment reflects the emphasis firms have placed on raising productivity to counter intensified global competition and near record-low profitability.

Phillip Cross,
Canadian Economic Observer,
2/93

Vendors/suppliers

Here is an unlikely source of pressure to downsize, but a source nonetheless. Vendors view you as their customers. You, as a customer, are demanding more, better, faster and cheaper from them just as your customers demand that from you. One way they might deliver on that demand is to do for you what in the past you may have had to do yourself. Vendor efficiencies and improvements can drive down work content and reduce the demand for people in your organization.

The idea is at least as old as Henry Ford and the Model T. Ford used to buy castings from a vendor who agreed, as a condition of being awarded an exclusive relationship with Ford, to package those castings in boxes made from a specified wood, cut, drilled and bolted together in a prescribed pattern. True, it was an expensive and somewhat bizarre packaging requirement but it guaranteed that this vendor would be profitable for years to come.

When the product arrived at the Ford plant, the boxes were disassembled and the parts, already cut, shaped and drilled, were positioned as the floorboards of a brand new Model T. This ingenious technique foreshadowed hundreds of ways for suppliers to make work less complex for their customers, reducing work content and the need for employees.

Shareholders/constituents

The vice-president for nuclear power generation of a major East Coast power company suggested shareholder pressure is a crucial external force. Why was his company having so much trouble shifting its focus from the short view to the long term?

Everyone in the executive suite recognized that a short-term focus was a disadvantage. The long view was the key to success. But they still kept doing short-term tasks and sacrificing the long-term good.

The answer: stock prices. Stock prices rise and fall by the minute. Any action that might result in even a momentary dip in price per share is discouraged. Long-term drops in price per share can result in senior managers being removed from office.

Stock price is the private sector analog to popularity polls for elected officials. Corporate officers, just like their elected counterparts in the public sector, are continually "running for re-election". In the private sector, a vote of "no confidence" can come at any time. The job is always at risk. Share price is one indicator of public confidence in the incumbent's job performance and, hence, job security.

Some strategies which might preclude the need for downsizing can produce short-term productivity shortfalls. Anything other than business as usual disrupts the organization and can drive down stockholder confidence and, thus, price per share. The same decision makers who feel at risk from any share price variations are reluctant to tinker with the organization.

Call it a blind spot, cowardice or lack of integrity. Call it simple self-interest. It is a human phenomenon. As a vice-president of a major U.S. railroad said, "Price per share drives everything. If I don't do whatever is needed to maintain the price per share the board of directors will simply get rid of me and replace me with someone who can."

Shareholders, through their agents and boards of directors, are making organizations risk averse by reacting to daily and hourly operational decisions rather than yearly and decade-long strategic visions. This short-term obsession is typical of analytical thinking. It ignores the realities of the overall system and prevents decision makers from being proactive.

A variation on the theme of shareholders and constituents as a force which encourages downsizing is the adoption of the organization by a new parent company. In today's organizational climate, most notably within the private sector, mergers and acquisitions are creating new constituencies. Ownership of organizations is transferred, and the consolidation of resources and/or elimination of duplication ensues.

Take the recent merger of Lockheed and Martin Marietta. A new company has emerged, and one of the predictable effects of that creation is pressure to realize the economic benefits of eliminating duplications in staff and support functions.

It is nearly impossible to identify a merger/acquisition that has not produced downsizing as a side effect.

This is also an issue in the public sector as functions are merged, reorganized or consolidated. The organizational parent may still be the public agency, but the reorganization yields the same pressures to reduce headcount as occurs in the private sector. Part of "reinventing government" is to consolidate functions and eliminate duplicate positions.

On the first anniversary of Vice-President Gore's report on reinventing government, President Clinton used the occasion to inform the American people that 71,000 federal positions had been eliminated in the first 18

All regions except British Columbia posted declines, reflecting a sharp contraction in primary industries and counted large cuts in Central Canada's manufacturing base.

Phillip Cross, *Canadian Economic Observer,* 2/93

months of his presidency. Reorganizations and realignments, the public analog to mergers and acquisitions, were credited with the elimination of those "unnecessary" positions.

It should be noted that in both the U.S. and Canada, pressures to reduce government spending, and thus headcount, can often result in a numbers game. Political opponents use varying schemes for slicing and dicing the data to alternately prove that large numbers of jobs were eliminated or that those jobs were merely relocated or hidden where they are less obvious. When politicians quote force reductions the numbers they cite should not necessarily be taken at face value.

Political entities/politicians

There are few who would argue that the political system does not influence organizational effectiveness. In the summer of 1994, for example, during the debates over the U.S. health care initiative, the Rand Institute estimated that employer mandates would result in 100,000 layoffs, as businesses cut headcount to control costs. Others, less sympathetic to the Clinton plan, were predicting a million or more layoffs if employer mandates were in the final bill.

Whether it is mandated safety, equal employment or strike resolution, politicians can drive the cost of doing business up or down.

Naturally, the impact of the political system is even more keenly felt in the public sector. An individual political appointee can initiate a restructuring or downsizing by fiat, especially at the state or provincial and municipal levels. Fiats also apply to the federal system. Vice-president Gore, in a single document, called for the reinventing of the U.S. government, including a massive resizing of several agencies, bolstering some and downsizing others.

Throughout Canada, the U.S. and Mexico, political aspirants at all levels have been running on the "government isn't working" platform for several decades. They campaign as change agents, and among "conservative" candidates, fixing government often equates to shrinking the size of the government employee pool.

In Newfoundland the provincial government recently announced plans to eliminate 27 school boards organized along religious lines and replace them with 10 regional boards. The elimination of 17 school boards was justified because it " . . . could save $10 million a year for the cash-strapped provincial government" according to Associated Press.

Finally, let's not overlook the judicial system. In a recent case involving General Motors the courts first awarded and then rescinded a $100 million punitive damages award. If upheld that award could have triggered a $500 million recall/buyback of the vehicles in question. The impact of that expense on the bottom line, and hence on the jobs of thousands of workers, cannot be ignored.

Regulators

Another powerful political arm that demands instant gratification is those agencies and departments with regulatory authority. Representing their own vested interests, they exert the demand for more, better, faster and cheaper in those arenas where they are granted regulatory authority.

Regulators have allowed, some say encouraged, regulated organizations to operate "fat and lazy" by limiting competition and relaxing anti-trust restrictions. When regulatory constraints are relaxed, or when whole industries are deregulated, as with transportation and communication, there is an almost immediate shift to "lean and mean". Competition will do that to an organization.

AT&T responded to deregulation in 1983 and divestiture of its operating companies in 1984 with an immediate downsizing. About a year after divestiture a friend working on the AT&T chairman's staff called to say she had just been promoted into the worst possible job. Her task was to develop the plan for cutting 27,000 people from the payroll that year, with the expectation that the cuts would keep coming at or near that rate for several years. The difference between then and three years earlier: deregulation and competition.

Net job reductions in what was formerly known as the Bell System during the 10 years following deregulation/divestiture were on the order of 250,000—25 percent of the original one million employee population of 1983.

Technology

No one can deny the impact of technology on the number of people needed to do a given job. Technology has been promising that machines could replace people since the earliest days of the Industrial Revolution. In the 1920s, Frederick Taylor's school of "scientific management" accelerated the process and at the same time took analysis to its greatest heights, the time and motion study. Work was reduced to its simplest tasks. Tasks were reduced to their simplest movements. Those tasks or subtasks that could be mechanized were. Those that could not, or could not be mechanized cheaply enough, were left for people to perform.

As technology developed, more and more tasks could be taken from people and given to machines. The promise was wealth and leisure for the masses. The reality was the dehumanization of the workplace where people were assigned repetitive tasks and treated by the organization as if they, too, were interchangeable parts of the assembly line. They were just the most expensive, least reliable and most temperamental machines on the line.

Jobs Lost in January 1994:

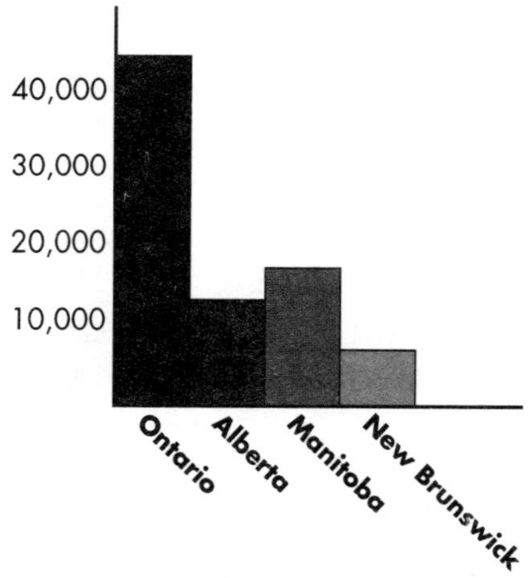

From statistics reported in the *Globe and Mail* 2/5/94.

Machines continue to replace people, causing some jobs to be eliminated. Yet some argue that for every job technology eliminates, technology creates two or more jobs to replace it. The statistics are confusing at best and are being effectively used to support both sides of the man versus machine argument.

That argument aside, some technology driven jobs, by their very nature, create both employment opportunities and inevitable job displacement. Consider keypunch operators. In the late 1960s and early 1970s keypunch operators were being told they represented the future. Keypunch operating was the entry to the wonderful world of computers. Where are the keypunch operators now? Korea, the Philippines, Costa Rica. They followed that old, expensive mainframe equipment that was exported to third world countries.

As far as most of the industrial world was concerned, here was a job created and eliminated by technological change in a span of 15 to 20 years. Whether you are pro- or anti-technology, there is no way an organization can avoid downsizing the keypunch department when the technology becomes obsolete. Yet, other jobs may be created so that from a net headcount perspective, there is no reduction in force.

Some downsizing is the result of technological change. But by the same token technological change creates new jobs. The problem for the organization and its employees is that the new jobs may not be available to the people who held the old jobs.

Domestic and foreign economic conditions

Remember NAFTA? What was it Ross Perot said in 1984? "There is going to be a great sucking sound heard throughout the U.S. as American jobs move to Mexico." Have you looked at the new Chevrolet Camero? The ads say, "What else would you expect from the country that gave you rock and roll?" What they don't say is, "Made in Canada." Bought a U.S. manufactured VCR lately? Or a TV or transistor radio? Own a Japanese car? What about the economic opportunities created by the emergence of capitalism in the former Soviet republics.

What this tells us is that the availability and costs of foreign labor pools, tax incentives offered by offshore governments, international tariffs and regulations that govern the markets and economies of foreign competitors are other external factors influencing which, and how many, jobs reside within which borders.

The desire to raise productivity and cut labor costs was one of the key determinants of labour market development in 1992. Output per person employed rose by 2.3 per cent in the business sector, after a 1.8 per cent increase in labour productivity in 1991. Manufacturers led the drive to boost productivity, as they faced the most intense global competition.

Phillip Cross,
Canadian Economic Observer,
2/93

With the passage of GATT and the formation of the emergence of the World Trade Organization some experts are expecting even more downsizing pressures on Canadian and U.S. organizations.

Unions and the labor pool

Unions also influence the size of the employee body for a given organization. They can exert pressure to maintain jobs through work rules and bargained-for staffing levels. As the economic pressure to resize mounts, layoffs and downsizing, training and retraining, out placement and early retirements all become bargaining issues.

The labor pool in a given community can also influence strategic decision making. It is no accident that Silicon Valley became the seat of computer development. Look at who lives, and gets educated, in that area. The rural southeastern U.S. has attracted manufacturing relocating from the North and East in part because of its traditionally non-unionized pool of workers who have a track record of good work without the added complexity of being organized.

As you can see, the external forces which motivate internal strategic decision making, including the decision to downsize, are numerous and complex. Their impact on the organization should not be underestimated. The above discussion merely suggests that the decision to downsize is not made in a vacuum. This choice cannot be fully understood by analyzing it in an environment-free laboratory. It is the environment itself which drives the decision. Therefore, it takes a systems view to understand why any particular organization downsizes.

The obvious answer to "Why downsize?" may be to cut costs. To address the more subtle aspects of the follow-up question "Why cut costs?" requires systemic thinking.

The myths and promises

Embedded in the decision to downsize are a number of beliefs and expectations. Decision making is a process of identifying a need for action, considering the various available alternatives and then selecting the best of the lot. The selection process usually includes some evaluation of the relative pros and cons for each alternative under consideration. That evaluation will always be based on a mixture of facts and more or less reasonable expectations based on best guesses.

Part of the motivation to downsize can be understood if we examine the promises implied by the decision and the myths surrounding downsizing as an organizational alternative.

Consider the following myths and what the data suggest may be contradictory realities.

David Noer, an expert in organizational behavior at the Center for Creative Leadership, says survivors often feel guilty because from their perspective it is arbitrary; they are no worthier than those who were fired, only luckier.

Under the circumstances it seems almost immoral to take much joy in work. So they become morose and cautious, worrying that they will be washed away in the next wave of discharges.

Lee Smith,
Fortune,
7/25/94

Myth—Downsizing is a one-time cost that can be calculated

Lee Iacocca popularized the term "bean counters" referring to people who use economic analysis as a primary basis for making business decisions. Downsizing has a number of fixed and predictable costs and benefits that can be anticipated. The problem with bean counting in this instance is the unanticipated and/or variable costs and the improbability of many of the anticipated benefits.

The only costs that can be predicted accurately are those associated with the people leaving the organization. There are numbers for the incented retirements, separation allowances, outplacement services and deferred pensions needed to remove people from the payroll. There are also wages and benefits costs, the "loaded" salaries of those who leave, which can be deducted from the fixed overhead of the organization after the downsizing.

The myth of predictable costs ignores the costs of overcoming employee anger and resentment, of coping with resistance and denial, of moving beyond blame and guilt. These costs are difficult to predict with any accuracy because they are based on the unique psychological reactions of employees to the highly personal experience of surviving a downsizing.

There are also costs associated with teaching employees new skills, transitioning supervisors into new roles and, in general, helping people adapt to a significantly changed status quo.

Myth—Downsizing will result in greater employee involvement, responsibility and risk taking

There is an assumption made by many downsizing organizations that there is "fat" in the organizational structure and inefficiencies in the way work is performed. There is a belief that employees do not always give a full day's effort for their pay, and that in the new, leaner, downsized organization, this will all change. Employees will accept responsibility for finding ways to do the job better, faster and cheaper. Employees will accept higher levels of responsibility, seeking and finding ways to do more with less. Employees will experiment with alternative work processes that promise unforeseen efficiencies, quality improvements and added value to each step in the flow of work.

The reality too often is that employees actively resist what they view as attempts by the organization to get more work from them for the same pay. They are angry with the organization for how it is treating them and are more inclined to sabotage new efforts than they are to support them.

They may also be increasingly risk averse, fearing that any failure at a time when people are being cut from the payroll could give the organization an opportunity to add yet another name to the list of those who will be leaving.

Myth—Downsizing will not change the essential nature of the organization

This myth presumes that every organization has an essential nature. It is safe to argue that every organization has a history which, if extended into the future, can predict certain tendencies. It is unrealistic to presume that this essential character will be unaffected by the decision to downsize, if downsizing represents a departure from the organization's history.

Downsizing is sometimes the pivotal event in redefining the organization's essential nature. Take Delta Airlines. Delta's organizational culture, its essential nature, like that of many established and traditionally stable organizations, was often described as that of a "family". That essential attribute was best expressed several years ago when Delta's employees raised enough money to purchase a Boeing 767, *The Spirit of Delta,* which they gave to their airline as a symbol of their loyalty and faith. This act of employee generosity is celebrated at a number of airports in the Delta Crown Room lounges. Commemorative pictures of *The Spirit of Delta* ceremony with snippets of the red ribbon that was tied around it are proudly displayed to remind Delta's business passengers that they are being cared for by a loving family, not an impersonal business.

This same airline decided in 1993 and 1994 to lay off thousands of employees. In the outplacement seminars presented to these employees the perception of Delta as a family was a subject of derision and the focus of a lot of anger. The choice to lay off "loyal" employees was a pivotal event and changed employees' and to some extent customers' perceptions of the essential nature of the organization. One laid-off pilot expressed it this way. "We're not a family. Families don't abandon their members when things get rough. Or if we are a family, we're a dysfunctional one."

Susan Barciella, writing for the Knight-Ridder newspaper syndicate, quotes one outplacement consultant as saying. "The corporation is not a family anymore. It's a team." Families hang together through better or worse, richer or poorer. Teams have a different nature. They release some members, recruit others and reshape, reassigning roles as the good of the team dictates." Unless the team model is your organization's essential nature, expect downsizing to alter it significantly.

One more common mistake: companies often spread out their downsizing efforts over months, even years. Worse still, some companies downsize repeatedly. An AMA study of 1,100 companies found that they sometimes come to view downsizing as a normal option rather than a desperate measure. "The best indicator of future downsizing is present downsizing," says Eric Greenber, editor of AMA Research Reports. *He adds that a "double dip" of downsizing is the norm.*

Warren Boroson
and Linda Burgess,
Across the Board,
11/92

Myth—Downsizing will result in an immediate improvement in financial performance

At best this is wishful thinking. It is more reasonable to expect a short-term increase in expenses, as the costs of the downsizing itself are amortized. There is a phenomenon which we have observed which we call the investment paradox.

What many organizations encounter immediately following downsizing is the need to increase their per employee investment, especially regarding new technology and training. While total costs may go down, per employee performance actually decreases as employees adapt to new tasks, increased workloads and the new methods needed to realize the eventual financial improvements promised by the downsizing.

There are also a number of unanticipated costs which can adversely impact financial performance if the surviving employees choose to resist the changing expectations and requirements set out by the organization. Employees can either actively or passively sabotage the reallocation of tasks and the requirement that work be done more efficiently and effectively. They can also redirect their creative energies away from solving organizational problems and in the directions of self-preservation and proving to management that the downsizing was a mistake.

Myth—Downsizing is a one-time correction of past mismanagement. We won't have to go down this road again.

That, too, is an unsafe assumption. Downsizing is a response to various subtle and ever-changing external influences. It is unrealistic to assume that it may never be appropriate again.

Organizations which claim that this was "it" may be seeking to appease their employees. The risk is that they may, in fact, have to repeat the downsizing exercise and, in that case, they stand to lose whatever credibility they might have with employees.

There is a corollary danger as well. Stating that the organization will never downsize again can encourage employees to adopt an entitlement mindset, believing that job security is a reality, and thus let go of some of the incentive they may otherwise experience to develop their skills and improve their work performance.

The only way a leader is going to translate vision into reality—an ability that is the essence of leadership—is to anchor and implement and execute that vision through a variety of policies, practices, procedures and systems that will bring in people and empower them to implement the vision.

Warren Bennis,
Executive Excellence,
11/94

Supporting strategies and tactics

As indicated above, downsizing does not occur in a vacuum. It is a response to a variety of complex and subtle external and internal forces. It is also typically accompanied by other cost-saving tactics as well as strategies for expanding market penetration/share such as: quality improvement initiatives, raised productivity standards, introduction of more productive technologies, budget cuts, capital investment limitations, introduction of new services, improved customer intelligence, and better service and product quality monitoring. Some of these initiatives serve as additional internal forces which encourage downsizing. For example, productivity improvements mean that fewer people are required to perform the same amount of work.

Downsizing is also not a monolithic tactic; that is, it is not a single process for reducing headcount. A number of strategies typically take place concurrently and in combination. Among the more frequently employed downsizing approaches are restructuring, reengineering, rightsizing, realignment, privatization, consolidation, centralization, decentralization, attrition, outsourcing, subcontracting and layoffs.

1. Restructuring

This strategy is used when jobs are combined or reporting relationships are redefined. Essentially, it redesigns the organization chart, but does little to change the way work gets done. It is based on the perceptions and insights of higher level management and can be useful in identifying people and positions that are no longer essential.

It is a quick and dirty solution to the problem, inexpensive to implement, but unlikely to be effective in the long term since it lacks a systemic view of the organization and is hampered by the decision makers' lack of objectivity.

2. Reengineering

This strategy takes the notion behind restructuring to its logical conclusion. Rather than set out to redesign the organization chart, it reexamines how work gets done. It starts with the organization's mission and redesigns individual jobs, work flows and interdependencies. In the process, nonessential work operations are identified and can be eliminated when doing so is strategically sound. The natural result is that the reengineered organization has simplified work processes and flows which require fewer people to carry them out. The net results, as with restructuring, also include a new organization chart, one that reflects fundamental changes in what work gets done and how the work gets done.

Its advantages are that it is systemic, comprehensive, and can be very effective. It is also expensive, difficult to do well and usually very time consuming, since it involves the use of external (objective) experts who go through detailed organizational analyses, reports, recommendations, etc.

Reengineering can also be a traumatic shock to the culture of the organization if the recommendations violate organizational traditions and norms. So while the proposed changes may be ideal on paper, rarely do they translate well into the real world. Reengineering works best with a committed and effective leader at the helm of the organization, one whose competence and motives are trusted by the rank and file.

While slow, expensive and difficult, from a systems point of view at least, this is the most appropriate approach to defining staffing requirements and determining if and how to downsize.

3. Rightsizing

Rightsizing is one of those euphemisms that some organizations use for any form of downsizing. They believe that putting the word "right" in the name will put a positive spin on what most people see as a negative process.

The "right" in rightsizing has to do with reevaluating the staffing requirements for the work at hand, reviewing how the work has evolved and determining if the work is being done properly and if the size of the current staff is appropriate. The depth and breadth of rightsizing initiatives range from superficial paper reviews of job descriptions and organization charts to in-depth work and staffing analyses.

As a euphemism rightsizing is a deception. It is a cowardly way to avoid the realities of downsizing, hiding behind the suggestion that this is somehow the "right" thing to do and therefore not subject to critical review.

As a reevaluation process it is a necessary but insufficient component of reengineering. To rightsize without considering the fuller context of moving from the organization's mission and the forces shaping it as a starting point, is inadequate.

4. Realignment

This is another term that is sometimes substituted for "restructuring". It usually refers to a redefined reporting relationship, taking a function out of one line of reporting and placing it in another. Most times the impact on total headcount is minimal. Sometimes it is a process for dealing with attrition (see below) such as the case where a manager retires and his/her groups are realigned so that they report to other, existing managerial entities. For example, if the sales manager from District A retires the district may be realigned, with various sales people and their territories and customers reassigned to other sales manager groups.

5. Consolidation, centralization and decentralization

These three processes seek to relocate where work is done and decisions are made. Consolidation seeks to combine job functions in a common reporting relationship. Centralization seeks to gain efficiencies by having separate functions share centralized staff support and direction. Decentralization seeks to make the organization more responsive and agile by placing support and decision-making responsibility in the various subentities.

All these structural choices can result in the elimination of some positions and as such are downsizing tactics.

None of these structures should be an end in itself. There is no inherent superiority in any of these structural choices. Each is better viewed as a means to some strategic goal. If being more responsive is a strategic goal, decentralizing those decisions which impact customer responsiveness or satisfaction might be in order. If consistent interpretation of policy is a strategic goal then centralization works well. If too many people are calling the same customers, or if internal competition is confusing the customer, then consolidation could fix that specific problem.

6. Attrition

This is the least painful form of downsizing to many decision makers since it does not require them to force anybody out of a job. It merely redistributes the workload formerly performed by the person leaving among those persons remaining.

When that workload is easily absorbed by the remaining workers it is a logical choice. When that added workload overloads the remaining workers it creates problems. People are under increased pressures. Priorities may become confused. Anger and resentment may motivate workers to be less effective.

Relying on attrition is a situational call. Look at the specifics and determine whether the redistribution of the work is reasonable. If so, it is a good choice. If not, it may still be a good choice, but it will require a significant investment for the value to be realized. The issues raised by attrition and redistribution are addressed in detail in Chapter 4.

7. Subcontracting

This is a downsizing strategy that is used widely in both the public and private sectors. When a government agency subcontracts with a private company to provide a given product or service we call that privatization. In the private sector we call it subcontracting or outsourcing. The rational is simple. Subcontracting lets the organization receive what it needs without the staffing, supervising, managing and hassles. It doesn't have to recruit personnel, deal with union grievances, or discipline those who fail to perform or show up late. That is the vendor's problem.

Layoffs are a means to an end; corporate strategy helps to define that end.

Joel Brockner, *California Management Review,* Winter 1992

The organization doesn't have to maintain the staffing levels if workload drops off. Neither does it have to worry about suppliers, inventories or capital investment.

In some cases it can be the best of all worlds and, according to John Naisbitt in *Megatrends*, the reliance on subcontractors is growing. The concept is also expanding beyond subcontracting at the level of an individual employee or for a short-term project. Whole functions, once performed by large numbers of full-time employees, are being contracted out.

Consider this example. A very large company in the southeast has 35,000 or more employees operating from 72 facilities in the metro area. It has traditionally maintained an internal mail service. After trimming and restructuring, the mail service is composed of 56 employees. They prepare letters and packages for shipping and receive and sort thousands of letters and parcels daily. They pick up and deliver mail within the larger offices and serve as couriers to the smaller locations.

A small, aggressive service company has just approached management with a very attractive offer. They will do everything that the current in-house mail service does. They guarantee that they will meet or exceed all current standards for quality, productivity, accuracy and safety. They will do all their own staffing, and acquire and maintain their own fleet of vehicles. They will provide everything necessary for the entire mail operation, except the floor space needed for the mailrooms in the various larger buildings. And they will do it all for 14 percent less than it costs the company to do the job using its own employees, equipment and vehicles.

How attractive is that offer? How secure are those 56 jobs?

8. Layoffs

Layoffs get the most attention when we talk of downsizing. For some, especially in the business media, downsizing means layoffs. *Business Week* freely interchanged the terms *downsizing, layoffs, staff reductions, shedding employees* and *cutbacks* along with several other euphemisms in their May 1994 cover story on downsizing.

Layoffs get the attention because they are the most dramatic and painful process for reducing headcount. This is not new. Layoffs have been a part of the business cycle for some industries since their inception. Consider defense industries. They routinely staff up and staff down as they win, complete or lose large contracts. That is the nature of their business. Supply and demand.

But for some fields of endeavor, layoffs are foreign. Civil service and regulated utilities had century-long histories of never laying off a single employee. Education was a growth industry following W.W.II so layoffs were few and far between. Some U.S. based manufacturers held on to decades-long monopolies until just recently, when foreign competition began to squeeze them out of what they came to consider "their" markets.

"I don't know of any senior managers who enjoy laying people off. You're dealing with people's lives and families and so forth. You don't do it easily," says Bob Boeckner of WIlliam M. Mercer, Ltd.

Chethan Lakshman, *The Financial Post,* 4/16/94

Layoffs are the crux of the downsizing issue because of their scope and impact. *Business Week* cites 615,186 layoffs in the U.S. in 1993. The projected rate exceeded 3,100 laid-off U.S. employees *daily* for 1994. Whole towns and cities reel when major layoffs are announced. Some towns are truly one-company towns. When that company lays off a significant number of employees, the economy of the whole town is undermined.

Some colleagues argue that layoffs are never called for. Jerry Harvey, author of the *Abilene Paradox,* in a presentation to a conference of organizational consultants several years back, talked about layoffs as unconscionable. They were never justified. The preferred alternative was to cut back everyone equally, to save all jobs and share the sacrifice. That is a noble sentiment but not likely to become *modus operandi* for organizations today. Even if you agree with Harvey's ideal, it is not likely to become your organization's reality. And not just because top management is selfish or greedy.

Sometimes the external forces described above are such that a factory cannot be saved, a product line cannot be continued and a workforce cannot be converted. Sometimes the real costs of retraining, refitting and adapting exceed the resources of the organization. Sometimes there is insufficient time or capacity for the changes needed to preserve jobs.

Sometimes downsizing, even layoffs, are the best right answer for the situation.

But make no mistake about it, layoffs are an expensive alternative. They cut some costs, notably wages and benefits, in the short run, but in the long term create other substantial costs. The key is to understand, before the fact, what each option offers. Know what the long-term costs are and make the decision based on facts rather than myths, half-truths and wishes.

Conclusion

Is downsizing *de facto* evidence of incompetent management? Is there validity in the argument that "They should have seen this coming" or "We never should have gotten this big in the first place?"

You can argue that downsizing is a symptom of incompetent management in certain cases. The obvious examples are those where management ignored the external forces and sustained the myths, while ignoring the less disruptive alternatives. The truth remains that those are the exceptions. In most cases downsizing is the painful alternative remaining after all else has been considered. It is the most difficult decision, because despite the perceptions of the cynics, most decision makers choosing to downsize are good people trying to do the right thing at the time.

Given the advantages of hindsight it is possible to second guess them, but the reality remains, in more cases than not, good people were doing their best to serve their organizations in difficult times with limited understanding of what was causing the events they faced.

Could they have done a better job of anticipating the future and preventing the disruptions caused by downsizing? Of course. We can always do better. Were they incompetent? Perhaps, to a degree. Is downsizing evidence of callousness or malice? Only rarely.

Downsizing is just another of the new realities facing everyone in the workplace. It is another form of change that we must all understand and manage. It is another variable in the organizational equation.

Natural history teaches us that species have to learn to adapt if they are to survive. Organizations and their employees have to learn to adapt to changing external forces if they are to survive. In the chapters which follow we discuss the nature of the change and suggest adaptations that will increase all our chances for survival.

Who will thrive in the new world?

- *Those who understand how the world works economically, ecologically and culturally.*
- *Those who re-invent themselves, who are mentally agile and willing to risk.*
- *Those who understand that loyalty no longer means having a job for life.*
- *Those who hone skills that set them apart from the crowd—who are forever learning.*
- *Those who can work in harmony with others—who respect and honor differences.*
- *Those who have an attitude of appreciation toward work—who regard work as a privilege not as an entitlement or a right.*
- *Those who seek to maximize their contribution—who have a clear sense of purpose.*
- *Those who are flexible—who can adapt rapidly to changing needs and circumstances.*
- *Those who keep commitments—who do what they say they will do, despite the obstacles.*
- *Those who take personal responsibility for their own success and happiness.*

David McNally, *Executive Excellence*, 3/94

Summary Map

The Downsizing Phenomenon

Downsizing clichés

"Reasons" given for downsizing:

- staying competitive
- getting lean and mean
- doing more with less

Reasons why organizations downsize

- Response to customer demands for more, better, faster, cheaper
- Pressure from competitors who cause customer demands to increase by exceeding their expectations
- Vendor efficiencies and improvements result in reduced organizational workforce needs (your vendors perform work steps previously done in your organization).
- Shareholder demands for greater return on investment; constituent demands for elimination of staff and support duplications resulting from mergers
- Government mandates and regulations which result in fewer positions
- Response to demands from regulatory agencies which result in layoffs to reduce expenses caused by the new regulations
- Technological advances that reduce the number of people needed to do a job
- Foreign labor, tariffs and regulations
- Union-bargained agreements regarding layoffs, downsizing, retraining and retention

Downsizing myths

- Downsizing is a one-time cost that can be calculated.
- Downsizing will result in greater employee involvement, responsibility and risk taking.
- Downsizing will not change the essential nature of the organization.
- Downsizing will result in an immediate improvement in financial performance.
- Downsizing is a one-time correction of past mismanagement.

Downsizing approaches

- Restructuring—jobs are combined; reporting relationships redefined.
- Reengineering—how work is done is reexamined; nonessential work operations are identified and eliminated.
- Rightsizing—how work is done and whether or not staffing is appropriate are reevaluated.
- Realignment—reporting relationships are redefined.
- Consolidation—job functions with a common reporting relationship are combined.
- Centralization—separate functions share centralized staff support and direction.
- Decentralization—support and decision-making responsibility is relocated to various subentities.
- Attrition—workload is redistributed when an employee leaves.
- Subcontracting—work is placed outside the organization.
- Layoffs—jobs are eliminated due to economic or other conditions.

Chapter 2

From Decision to Implementation

It is not sufficient for management to merely recognize the forces which lead to downsizing. Nor is it enough for the organization to understand some of the mechanisms available for reducing headcount. This knowledge and understanding must be supplemented with the skills to make the correct decision, announce it and implement it effectively. These three components of downsizing—deciding, announcing and implementing—deserve detailed individual consideration.

The decision to downsize, by whatever means, presumes a rational process. It is appropriate to question whether the processes commonly used to make this decision are adequate for the task.

How the decision is to be announced to the various stakeholders is one component of the overall process which is too often mismanaged to the detriment of the subsequent implementation. The strategy for announcing the downsizing decision merits more deliberation than it is typically afforded.

The overall strategy for implementing the downsizing itself is the most critical determinant of its eventual success. A poorly conceived downsizing strategy, well implemented, is probably better for the organization than a brilliant strategy, poorly implemented. *Fortune* magazine several years ago noted that 90 percent of strategic plans fail due to poor implementation. Our experience suggests that as many as 90 percent of all downsizings fail to achieve their strategic goals due to poorly conceived and executed implementation strategies. This is where we will devote the most attention as we explore the decision to downsize.

Making the decision

In Chapter 1 we discussed some of the forces behind the decision to reduce the number of employees. Let's review the decision-making process and identify which steps and substeps in that process need special attention when the decision under consideration concerns downsizing.

There is an intuitive decision model that may help illustrate the process as it is used in most organizations. Whatever model is employed, it can be captured in the following six steps.

Step 1–Identify the problem

What is the essential nature of the situation that is causing you to respond by making a decision? What is the difference between the current state of the organization and the expected or desired state? Why is that of concern to you?

This is a diagnostic step. As the medical profession has noted, prescription without diagnosis is malpractice. What is called for in this step is a clear statement of what is wrong. The process of defining the problem benefits from being filtered through a series of discriminating questions, such as:

- What is the status quo?
- What is it about the status quo that is unsatisfactory?
- What is the desired alternative state?
- What is to be gained by moving from the status quo to the desired alternative state?
- Does changing the current state create any inconsistencies with this organization's stated policies or positions?
- Are there any legal or ethical considerations that would be adversely impacted by changing the current state?

When the forces of change described in Chapter 1 converge on the organization, the problem statement will often include reference to the need to drive down the cost of doing business. If the definition of any part of the problem includes a reference to costs, then the next logical extension of the problem statement may include the view that there are "too many people" since people costs are among the highest and fastest rising fixed costs in many organizations. Once "too many people" becomes part of the problem statement, downsizing emerges as the natural and logical response. The desired future state becomes an organization with fewer employees, with smaller human-resources-based overhead. As soon as cost is identified as part of the problem, downsizing is included in the vision of the future state.

Whatever the forces of change exerting pressures on the status quo, the problem statement needs to be expressed in broad enough terms to allow inclusion of a variety of alternative solutions. The problem definition should address the status quo of the entire affected system. Wherever possible the definition of what needs to be changed should be couched in terms which do not predefine the solution. Failing to define the problem broadly guarantees that some of the most productive alternative solutions will be excluded from consideration. After all, how you define the problem determines where you look for solutions.

The message of the marketplace is hard and unforgiving: keep adapting or be prepared for poor performance, even extinction. Change has to be on-going and relentless, a quasi-permanent state, because the business environment of tomorrow will change even faster than it's changing today. We will need to scramble more and more to keep up. Today's radically new structure easily becomes tomorrow's bureaucracy.

William L. Weiss,
Executive Excellence,
4/94

One way to ensure a broad definition of the problem is to maintain a systems view of the organization. View the problem in terms of how it impacts the organizational system as a whole, not just the subsystem where the majority of the symptoms appear.

The need to reduce the cost of doing business, for example, is not just about controlling the expenditure of resources. It touches every aspect of the organization. It has a ripple effect through the organization's environment, impacting customers, suppliers, competitors, unions and the community where the organization is located. Reducing the real cost of doing business can affect the relative value and/or availability of other, less tangible, resources such as the organization's reputation among investors. It changes the organization's history and may create new opportunities or threats which redefine the organization's ability to realize its mission. Cost reductions may require that the mission be redefined and will certainly affect the organization's ability to achieve strategic goals and the viability of existing strategic plans.

Once again the Nadler model provides a framework for ensuring that the definition of the problem is sufficiently systemic to allow for effective resolution. By examining the interdependencies and congruencies or fits between the system's components the model helps anticipate the likely results of a change in any one component. So if downsizing results in reduced resources, Nadler's OPM can help the decision maker predict what impact that might have on the organization's ability to do its work and achieve its goals.

One possibility that escapes some organizations in this step is that the problem can always be redefined. If the definition of the problem is too narrow, redefine it more broadly. If the definition limits the number of available alternative solutions, recast it. One technique that creative problem solvers have used for years when confronted with a problem that defies resolution or which can only be resolved by actions that the decision maker is trying to avoid, is redefinition. "If you can't solve the problem you have, change it to one that you can solve."

Defining the problem as "too many people" can only lead to one set of solutions: alternative strategies for reducing the number of people. If the problem is couched in terms relating to "the costs of doing business" or " the need to be more competitive" or " the need to be more attractive to potential investors" then other strategies can be included in the definition of the desired future state, and a whole new world of alternatives becomes available to the decision maker.

The more broadly the problem is defined the more alternatives become available. Of course, taken to its illogical conclusion, this process of problem redefinition results in a problem statement so broadly couched as to be irrelevant.

The key in Step 1 is to be very aware of how the problem is defined. How you define the problem in Step 1 determines where you will look for solutions in Step 2. The desired outcome here is a problem statement that sufficiently defines the difference between the status quo and the desired state without precluding any viable solutions from consideration.

Step 2–Identify alternatives

What options are available to you as you try to move from the current state to the desired state? What alternative courses of action might help you move closer to your goal?

This is a creative step. It requires that the decision maker be free to consider all alternatives that can produce the desired result. Step 2, defining possible courses of action, is only hampered by any attempt to evaluate these alternatives before all that can/should be identified have been identified.

"Premature evaluation" is a common disorder which results in only the most obvious alternatives being considered. It shuts down the creative process too early. Tactics such as brainstorming increase the likelihood that you will identify more, rather than fewer, viable alternatives. Creative processes for identifying additional alternatives have been well researched and documented. Books like Roger von Oech's *A Whack on the Side of the Head* suggest a wealth of techniques for identifying the less obvious alternative. The techniques are widely accessible, but unfortunately, underutilized by decision makers who find the easy alternative, the time honored solution, too hard to resist and the untried solution too uncertain to dare.

Senior management needs to recognize that a holistic or systemic approach must accompany an improvement initiative to give the desired more-for-less-result.

Arthur G. Davis,
Paper, Film & Foil Converter,
6/94

The primary filtering questions used in this step are:

- What other alternatives might we consider?
- What other alternatives does the definition of the problem allow, even if at first blush they are not "reasonable"?
- What else can I do to identify those solutions that aren't apparent to me yet?

The key to this step, and in Step 1, is to avoid the obvious. Do not necessarily dismiss it. Sometimes the obvious is a good answer. Just do not allow yourself to be limited by it and the definition of the problem it suggests. In cost-cutting situations, for example, reducing the number of employees is the obvious solution. It is the "easy" answer in that downsizing is the easiest alternative to think of. It may be a right answer in that it could accomplish the immediate goal. That does not make downsizing the best right answer in many cases, because, as we will find out in Step 3, the costs of downsizing are not well understood and the long-term problems it creates might well outweigh the short-term benefits it provides.

So how many alternatives should you identify? All that the significance of the decision deserves. The broader the ramifications of the problem, the more creative energy needs to be expended in ensuring that all the right answers that can be considered, get considered.

Step 3–Evaluate the alternatives

Step 3 is where each viable alternative is examined both analytically and systemically. The nonviable alternatives can be dismissed out of hand. For example if one alternative is to do nothing, and it is always an alternative, it may be dismissable if its implementation would produce unacceptable consequences. So the first systemic screening questions in the evaluation of alternatives are:

- What are the likely consequences of the alternative being considered?
- Are they acceptable?

If the likely consequences are not acceptable the alternative needs to be set aside. We only need to analyze those alternatives that are likely to produce acceptable consequences.

Once the field of alternatives being considered is reduced to only those whose likely consequences could be acceptable, we are ready for the remaining screening questions:

- What will happen if we implement this alternative?
- What will it take to implement this alternative?
- How likely is it that this alternative will succeed?
- What possible negative ramifications might this alternative produce?
- What will happen if we attempt this alternative and it is not effective?
- What other information do we need before we can determine if this alternative is desirable? Optimal?
- How will we get that information?

Imbedded in this line of questioning is an assumption. The process of screening each alternative assumes that the persons doing the screening can adequately differentiate between what they know and what they do not know. That seems so obvious and so simple that it amazes people to learn that one of the biggest contributors to poor decision making is the failure to make that distinction.

All of us have a difficult time distinguishing between what we know, *for a fact*, and what we have come to believe based on prior experience, indirect information or faith. For example, it is widely believed that reducing the number of people in the organization will reduce the direct costs of labor by a predictable amount. In fact, it is argued, that amount can be accurately computed based on the salary and benefits of those who will leave, minus the costs of outplacement, retirement incentives, lump sum settlements and other termination allowances. Reality is that the actual savings rarely match those that were projected in this step of the decision-making process. There are uncertainties in most downsizing strategies that make the predictions suspect.

What often happens is that the direct cost of salary and benefits goes down less than anticipated. In some cases it has even been known to go up. Net costs of salary and benefits can rise for a number of reasons. Imagine that we now have fewer people doing the same amount of work. Some efficiencies are realized but overtime hours increase. We are now paying time and a half or double time for some of the same work that only cost straight time prior to the downsizing. Not only is salary cost per unit of work affected, so too is the stress level of the employees working all that overtime. Increased stress leads to increased susceptibility to illness and, voilà, absenteeism and benefit costs go up. To fill the gaps in the production capacity, temporary employees are brought in, often at a higher short-term cost than regular employees.

A 1992 American Management Association survey of 547 companies that downsized last year showed that profits improved for just 43.5 percent.

Christopher Ryan,
Ingram's,
9/93

The point is not that downsizing does not produce cost savings. It usually does. Just note that as decision makers we are not always very adept at distinguishing between what we know for a fact and what we expect, believe or wish for.

Knowing the difference between what we know and what we cannot say with certainty is a critical element in the process of evaluating alternatives.

Step 4–Select the optimal alternative

The key word here is "optimal". It is useful to differentiate between an optimized solution and a maximized solution. Optimizing is a systemic concept. Russell Ackoff, in a presentation to AT&T senior management, illustrated with an automotive example the difference between optimizing and maximizing. The best engine in the world, mounted to the best chassis in the world, running through the best transmission in the world with the best coach work in the world does not necessarily produce the best car in the world. The parts may not fit well enough to make a car that can even run. What makes the best car is when a very good engine, transmission, chassis and coach are well suited to each other and when the interrelationship of the components is such that each part produces the ideal contribution to the whole. Optimizing is about a series of trade-offs and complements which produce a harmonious and effective whole.

The optimal decision is the one that best serves the whole organization. It is the best fit for the interrelationships between the organization's environment, history, resources, mission, vision, values, goals, objectives and ongoing action plans. The optimal decision is both strategically and systemically sound.

The critical screening questions in selecting the optimal alternative concern the congruence between the probable post-decision organizational state and the most desirable post-decision state. It is a comprehensive look at the consequences of the decision on the whole system and its containing environment, not just on a single subsystem.

- How will this decision move us closer to the desired state?
- What are the likely outcomes that will move us further away from the desired state?
- Is the net result sufficient progress towards our desired future to warrant the costs?

Step 5–Implement the decision

Once the decision is made, implementation is the next step. This is perhaps the biggest stumbling block to success. Is seems that more harm is done by good decisions, poorly implemented, than by bad decisions. The reason is simple. People pay attention to bad decisions and, in most organizations, someone will have the insight and courage to point out that a decision is or was bad.

Poor implementation is less obvious. What typically happens is that a good decision, poorly implemented, is declared a bad decision. There are far fewer poor decisions out there than we suspect. Many of the decisions that we have labeled bad, are really quite appropriate decisions that were clumsily or ineptly implemented.

Consider the decision several years ago to eliminate 20 typists in a word processing center (typing pool), by creating an administrative support service group comprised of 18 or so private secretaries assigned to midlevel managers. This was seen as a good application of then current technology as a vehicle to increase efficiencies and reduce costs.

The decision was sound. The implementation was thoughtless and amateurish. Plan one was to fire the typists. Give the existing secretaries word processing computers. Place them in a central pool. Have them all report to a single administrative supervisor.

Eighteen midlevel managers would lose their dedicated secretaries. They would also lose the confidence that comes with having immediate access to a needed resource, the control over that person's priorities, the comfort that comes from an established relationship, and the ease of assigning work knowing that their personal idiosyncrasies and those of their particular work would be satisfied. They also lost the status of having their own support person.

The secretaries lost the status of being a private secretary to an "important" manager. They were reduced (at least in their own minds) to pool typists, a position most had outgrown 20 years earlier. Plus they had to instantly master a challenging and, to some, intimidating new technology that the clerks being dismissed had already mastered.

The word processing clerks lost their jobs.

Worst of all, the decision was announced on Friday afternoon, to be effective the following Monday morning, with no warning or input from either the managers, secretaries or clerks and, supposedly, no recourse. If you were dissatisfied or thought there might be a better way to accomplish the goal, you were to keep that to yourself.

This decision was heralded as a cost savings, thus good for the company. Therefore, every employee was expected to support it out of a sense of teamwork and loyalty.

What actually occurred was a minirevolution. Forty or more managers, secretaries and clerks descended on the vice-president who made the decision, demanding that he reconsider. He did. This good decision was judged to be a horrid decision because the implementation strategy failed to address the peripheral issues surrounding the need to reduce headcount.

The staff consultant brought in to unravel this Gordian knot suspended the implementation of the decision and reimplemented it over the next three weeks, relying heavily on input from those affected. He listened to their concerns and addressed those concerns in an implementation strategy that allowed for a thoughtful and deliberate transition. The end result was 99

The remaining employees will draw their own conclusions about the company's fairness and trustworthiness. If separations are handled properly.

Lewis Kravitz,
Business Altanta,
12/93

percent consistent with the earlier decision. The only real difference was to take advantage of the flexibility inherent in the new technology and allow the secretaries to be linked electronically, but to remain physically situated where they had always been, just outside the managers' doors.

The essential decision was kept intact. Twenty positions were still eliminated. The services were overseen by an administrative supervisor. The new technology was introduced. The difference was in how the key elements of the original decision were implemented.

The key screening question in implementation is about how to minimize resistance to the change inherent in the decision while preserving the essential change itself.

Again, systemic thinking allows us to anticipate where resistance is likely to reduce the probability of a successful implementation. It foreshadows the impact of the decision on all affected subsystems and allows the decision maker to consider implementation strategies and tactics that address resistance to change, whether motivated by uncertainty and fear or by a personal or political agenda.

Step 6–Evaluate the decision

- Did it work?
- Did it produce the desired results?
- Did it produce any unanticipated (desirable or undesirable) results?
- What can we learn to make the next decision better?

It is well recognized that decision making has a learning component to it. By systematically examining the consequences of a decision we learn how to make better decisions in the future. We call this "experience". It is essential that we ask all the right questions if we are to optimize the learning inherent in experience. It is also necessary to ask these questions because rarely does a decision produce all the desired outcomes, none of the undesired outcomes or only those outcomes which were predicted.

By remembering to look at unanticipated outcomes, be they positive or negative, we can better our understanding of how the organizational systems really work. The most important learning, therefore, can be around the questions of why unanticipated outcomes were produced and what that means to future decisions. Another way of stating this is to ask how the new state differs from the desired or expected state. In other words, what new problems did the decision create?

In downsizing situations, one of the most common unanticipated results is the realization that the costs of downsizing were underestimated, especially those costs associated with the reactions to the decision by the survivors of the downsizing. These costs are discussed in Chapter 4 in some detail in an effort to allow tomorrow's decision makers to benefit from the experience of yesterday's decisions.

Implementing the decision

There appear to be three keys to the effective implementation of a change in how an organization accomplishes its work, such as a downsizing. Again, David Nadler has provided a model. In his application of the Organization Performance Model (OPM) to organizational change Nadler identified these three issues:

- resistance to the change from those employees who are affected
- the need for the systemic management of the transition from the current state to desired state
- the political issues raised as a change realigns the power bases of key leaders

Managing resistance

Resistance is a natural response to unsolicited and often unwelcome change. Questions which might help surface resistance reduction strategies include:

- How do we wish to manage the release of specific information about the implementation strategy? Who should we tell? What should we tell them? When should we tell? How should we tell them?
- How do we communicate this decision in ways that minimize resistance?

- Who should we involve in defining the implementation details? Whose support is essential for success? How do we earn that support? Whose opposition is likely to produce failure? How do we overcome that opposition?

Implementation oversight

To attempt a downsizing without a predetermined, deliberate and thoughtful implementation strategy is foolishness. One of the most important steps in developing and carrying out that strategy is the formation of a working group which will be responsible for the implementation. This team, ideally, would consist of representatives of all affected constituencies. This is the team charged with anticipating the ramifications of the decision to downsize and with developing the plans to achieve the desired results. Some of their agenda is obvious:

- Who will be responsible for managing which details of this transition?
- How will we define success in this venture?
- How will we measure the effectiveness of the implementation strategy?
- How will we deal with unanticipated outcomes?

Given a specific set of organizational objectives and authority to include downsizing as a means of achieving all or part of that set of objectives, the team will recommend how they might best be achieved:

- How do we determine how extensive the downsizing must be to achieve the desired results?
- How do we identify the positions that will be eliminated?
- How do we identify the individuals who will be told to leave?
- How do we encourage people to leave voluntarily?
- How much time will we allow for the process to unfold?
- What costs are associated with this decision?
- What transitional benefits do we choose to offer those who are leaving?

Political issues

The political questions are also important. They deal with those who have the political clout to cause the implementation strategy to fail either through active opposition or passive resistance, as well as those whose support is necessary for success.

- Whose support will this decision need?
- How can we earn the support of those whose support is critical? What reasons can we give them that will cause them to support this decision?
- Whose resistance would sabotage this decision?
- How can we neutralize critical resistance from those who oppose this agenda on political grounds?

These, and others like these, are the obvious questions that any downsizing raises. Addressing these questions within an implementation strategy is necessary, but not sufficient, to ensure an optimal implementation.

There is no correct set of responses to these questions. There is, as of yet, no proven formula which clearly states "Do this. Don't do that." for an effective implementation of the downsizing decision. Among that set of questions, however, there is some guidance we can infer from the experiences of others.

Announcing the decision—who, what, when and how to tell

In the case cited earlier, the organization's vice-president announced a reorganization of the secretarial and administrative support functions on the Friday evening before the Monday morning the decision was to be effective. This was a time honored, albeit ineffective, strategy for announcing a change. But that is not the worst announcement example.

A policy of candor and two-way communications with employees, built over the past six years, is helping Boeing weather this storm. As in many successful companies, the CEO is directly involved in giving employees and the rest of the world the bad news, with an emphasis on employees finding out first. Managers, who received the information the day before the public release, announced it to their employees at 7 a.m., the start of the shift. The public announcement was made at 11 a.m.

Michael J. Major, *Public Relations Journal,* 12/93

In August 1994 the evening news heralded the merger of Lockheed and Martin Marietta, two U.S. defense giants. There was talk of how the two complemented each other and of the strong, viable new company that would emerge. That evening *The MacNeil-Lehrer News Hour* had the usual panel of experts and analysts dissecting the merger. One of the experts announced that there would inevitably be layoffs. In fact, he pointed out that one of the more powerful motives behind mergers and acquisitions was the potential to eliminate duplications of efforts and trim staff.

If you were a Lockheed or Martin Marietta employee watching that newscast, you might have just heard the first public pronouncement that your job was in immediate jeopardy. From the employees' perspective, hearing potentially bad news through the media *is* the worst possible way for information of this significance to be communicated. What makes it so bad is the disrespect it communicates. The unspoken message is that "We do not care enough about you and how this decision could affect you to take the time or make the effort to let you know before we told the world." Yet, public announcements by third party observers seem to be the most common strategy for notifying employees of the next downsizing. Public announcements and the subsequent speculation are the worst strategy imaginable.

Consider just some of what is wrong with this approach.

What better fodder for the grapevine to chew upon that an "expert opinion", delivered through the media, that downsizing is inevitable. With no basis in fact, speculation will run rampant. Every individual and group insecurity will feed on the expert's guarantee that heads must roll. Even if the announcement of the merger in the Lockheed-Martin Marietta case had been shared with employees before it made the evening news, this added tidbit about the inevitability of downsizing would keep the grapevine fully occupied for months.

Organizational anxiety already exists. Employees are already concerned about the rapid rate of change in today's organizational climate. That concern is compounded by the personal and professional insecurities that most of us bring to the workplace. Together these concerns guarantee that a significant number of employees already experience a heightened sense of anxiety about their job security.

The inept introduction of the possibility of an imminent downsizing, without benefit of any official position or particulars, guarantees that those who had a little anxiety will now have more. For those who were already distracted from their work by a higher level of concern, anxiety now grows into paranoia.

Employees need to feel a recommitment to the firm after a restructuring.

Lewis Kravitz,
Business Altanta,
12/93

A colleague once noted that "it is impossible to overestimate the paranoia in most organizations". A decision is made in headquarters, and some employee in the farthest boondocks cries out, "Why are they doing this to me?"

If we define paranoia as the unreasonable fear that "they" are out to get you, then the inept introduction of the possibility of downsizing into the anxiety stew that many employees feast on daily can shift an already high level of anxiety over the brink from reasonable to unreasonable fear, to organizational paranoia.

There is no accounting process that can accurately capture the costs of the thousands of hours lost to gossip and speculation, distraction and diverted attention. It is more than the time spent at the water cooler. Think of the lost productivity, the simple and unnecessary errors made. Consider the costs as distracted employees let their minds wander from the task at hand to concerns for their futures, wrestling with a thousand "what ifs" in the wake of the media expert's pronouncement that "layoffs are sure to follow".

There are still other reasons why media announcements are to be avoided. In addition to the message of disrespect and the costs of speculation and distraction there is the perceived loss of control. When the media are used as management's spokesperson, one possible interpretation is that the media knows better than management what is going on.

During the days just preceding the 1984 Bell System divestiture, one manager defined the impact of "media first" communications this way: "Every time I read another speculation in the paper or hear another TV reporter tell us what management is going to do, before management has told us what they were going to do, I get the image of a train hurtling down the track at 100 miles per hour with no one in the engineer's seat."

Relying on the media to carry the message also suggests cowardice. Management gives the appearance of lacking the courage to tell the difficult truths to deserving employees, choosing instead to announce their intentions to "neutral" media representatives who will carry the bad news to the masses. The implied message is that management is hiding. Therefore, it is reasonable (or at least likely) to suppose that management has reason to hide, that the decision to downsize is somehow indefensible or unconscionable.

How many hours of productivity are consumed by speculation and anxiety in the aftermath of media prediction that downsizing is inevitable? How much do the perceptions of disrespect and of management incompetence, which come from the use of the media as management's speechmakers, cost the bottom line? No one has been able to accurately compute the costs of a poor announcement strategy. At best all we can do is intuitively and anecdotally to assert that the cost is real, significant and unnecessary.

What is the alternative to the announcement strategies described above?

- Tell employees before the decision is announced to the general public.
- Anticipate the speculations and concerns and answer their questions regarding who, when and how.
- Offer assurances of full and comprehensive ongoing communication surrounding the decision and its implementation.
- Assure employees that they will be the first to hear news relating to this decision.
- Then deliver on these promises.

Yes, there is a risk in sharing this form of information with employees. Some employees whom you are hoping would stay with the organization might view this as a sign that they should seek their fortunes elsewhere. Others might figure that since they have no future with the organization there is no value in putting forth extra effort. But the price paid for allowing employees to rely on the misinformation and speculation that accompanies the earlier illustrations of information mismanagement is inevitably higher.

Employee involvement

One proven tactic for reducing employee resistance to change has been to co-opt resistant employees by making them part of the team which defines the implementation strategy. This is the "lemonade" gambit, as in, "When life hands you lemons, make lemonade." Rather than allow them to stand to the side and criticize the decision and to snipe at your efforts to make the decision succeed, involve them in the implementation.

It would be ideal if all the potential resistors could be involved in making the initial decision. That is rarely practical. It can be prudent though if the employee in question is one of those with enough clout to foil the plan, if they are one of those key players whose support or, at a minimum, whose nonresistance is critical for decision approval and success. But most of the time, the best that can be hoped for is to involve enough employees in the implementation so that resistance is minimized, and perceptions of the decision, the organization and its leaders remain positive.

AT&T's American Transtech is an example of the lemonade gambit taken to its highest plane. According to Susan Richards, who was their VP of Human Resources at the time, Transtech was unique. Susan shared her experiences at the Positive Employee Practices Institute's annual conference in October of 1992.

Four guidelines that management can follow to help keep downsizing on track:

- *refocus on satisfying the customer*
- *core competencies*
- *integrate*
- *rework the core processes*

Arthur G. Davis,
Paper, Film & Foil Converter,
6/94

Created as a stock transfer agency to assist AT&T's shareholders through the 1984 divestiture, Transtech never expected the AT&T transfer services function to be a "permanent" organization. In July of 1991 management announced that Transtech would be going out of the AT&T share owner services business in September of 1992. The next fourteen months would require that the 400 share owner services employees be reassigned or terminated while maintaining appropriate service levels until the last day of business.

At the time of the announcement Transtech was the largest stock transfer agency in the world, processing 75 million share owner transactions annually. Throughout the transition period they would continue to meet their legal requirements, demonstrate commitment to their values and transition their business so that customer service never suffered. Through all this they committed to treat their employees so that everyone viewed the processes as fair.

Their strategy was driven by a mission focused on giving employees the resources to make personal choices for career opportunities and job continuity while maintaining the organization's commitment to service quality.

Transition management was a group effort. Committees and subcommittees were formed to ensure that the downsizing went according to plan. One of the transition team's subcommittees dealt with keeping employees informed about the business transition. Others identified service issues.

If employees believe management just expects them to continue with "business as usual" or expects them to simply be "happy to have a job" life after downsizing could be quite difficult.

Lewis Kravitz, *Business Altanta,* 12/93

About one third of the affected employees were re-deployed within Transtech. Another third found their way into other AT&T companies. The remaining third resigned, retired in the interim period or were separated.

The reason Transtech is held up as a model is that, up to the last day, service quality was maintained, employee morale stayed high and more so than in any other documented case, the typical negative aftermath of the decision to downsize was prevented by an effective implementation strategy based heavily on employee involvement.

Transition manager

To attempt a downsizing without giving a single person oversight responsibility is too common a mistake. One person has to know that it is his or her responsibility to monitor and track the implementation of the decision and to identify the attainment of redefined, critical, interim milestones and to be on the lookout for unanticipated outcomes.

That is not to say that this person is solely responsible for an effective implementation, merely that they are the single point of contact for all implementation related information, communication and activities.

The value of transition managers cannot be overstated. It becomes their job to keep one eye firmly focused on the transition. They are not allowed to be distracted from this task by other business exigencies. They are the early warning system when the unexpected inevitably happens. It is the transition manager's primary responsibility to notice when things go wrong, when the actual state of affairs differs from that which was predicted or that which is desired. They are the problem identifier, the diagnostician and the klaxon sounding the alarm.

To be effective in the role the transition manager must have:

- management's ear
- time to pay attention to the transition
- authority to sound the alarm

It becomes the transition manager's responsibility to ensure that the implementation strategy has adequate feedback mechanisms for monitoring and responding to unanticipated outcomes. That means that, like any other project, downsizing requires the systematic identification of action steps, outcomes, milestones and success criteria.

Any number of project management techniques may be applied. No single technique has proven itself superior. As a minimum it is helpful, however, to apply the RASI model to all action items necessary for the implementation.

RASI is an acronym standing for:

R = Responsibility. Who is responsible for doing the item being considered? Who is accountable for the successful and timely execution of the designated task?

A = Approval. Whose approval is needed for the action to be taken? This also includes approval authority for the allocation of the resources needed to perform the designated task(s).

S = Support. Whose help will be needed to complete the designated item? What form is that support likely to take?

I = Information. Who needs to be kept informed of the decision to perform the designated task and monitor its progress as it is being implemented?

Downsizing as a positive message

Whether you are the decision maker, the transition manager or the line manager whose workforce just got cut, stop saying, "I'm sorry." At some point continuing to apologize is tantamount to announcing to the world that you disagree with the decision. It is one thing to regret the negative impact of the decision on the lives of your employees It is quite another to undermine everyone's confidence in the decision and reduce its likelihood for success by holding it up for criticism, second guessing and disagreement.

If the decision was made for the right reasons then those reasons need to be communicated clearly and persuasively, perhaps more than once. But at some point, sooner better than later, the organization needs to treat the decision as a necessity, a fact of organizational life, a new reality in a changing world. Apologize to those whose careers are being disrupted. Express regrets that any employee has to suffer. Acknowledge that the decision, while necessary and correct, is hurtful to some. Then get on with it.

It is critical for the psychological well being of those who will be leaving, those who remain and, perhaps most especially, for those who made the decision and have to carry it out to move beyond grieving the decision and its consequences. At some point the grieving process has to stop and the organization has to get on with its business.

As we will see in Chapter 4, each supervisor and manager must be aware of this natural grieving process that the survivors of downsizing will experience and must be available to help employees move through it successfully. To keep returning to the "I'm sorry" stage is to retard that process, to hinder the organization's progress and to undermine the implementation of the decision. It suggests that the decision was somehow wrong, and that perception can keep employees focused on why they are entitled to resist this new reality rather than help them move towards adaptation to a new status quo.

Ethics issues

As mentioned above, one of Transtech's concerns throughout its downsizing was to ensure that the processes for implementation reflected the organization's stated values. This is another example of how it should be done.

Anytime an organization chooses to downsize it has made a decision rife with ethical content. Most evident to employees is that they are being threatened with a loss of employment which flies in the face of the stated position of most organizations to value and respect their employees. To most employees downsizing, almost by definition, feels like being disrespected and devalued.

Furthermore, there is the issue of fairness. Whether stated or implied, fairness is a key operational value for most organizations and employees. The fairness issue is deeply rooted in what we call the social contract of work. There has been an unspoken rule in our society that the only people who lose their jobs are those who fail to deliver "a fair day's work for a fair day's pay." Layoffs, even in industries where layoffs or furloughs are the norm, are temporary.

The most recent count notes that nine million U.S. workers permanently lost their jobs in the period from 1991 through 1993. These are not temporary setbacks. These people were "let go". They were told to find another job. Their services were no longer required. The most overwhelming response of these nine million has been, "It's not fair." These employees do not feel that their dismissal was a direct result of anything they personally did or failed to do. They were doing what was expected, required and condoned. They were, therefore, unprepared for the sudden reality of downsizing and believe that it is neither their fault, nor is it fair.

In the past 10 years, the question of ethics was not put forward. The message to chief executives from downsizing specialists is simple: being honest and open with staff can only benefit a company. Says Dick Cappon with Sobeco Ernst & Young.

Chethan Lakshman,
The Financial Post,
4/16/94

The fairness issue is exacerbated when downsizing coincides with overall organizational success or profit. For many there is a belief that downsizing is morally offensive and should be avoided at all costs. To downsize, while profitable, says to those who share this perception that the organization does not value its employees, or at least that it values them less than profit.

An alternative perception is that downsizing is a strategic, future-oriented decision that is equally appropriate whenever the organization's environment, resources and history require the organization to adapt to change. Profit is part of the resources and history but is not, in and of itself, sufficient to preclude the need for downsizing when forces in the environment call for change.

The ethical considerations of the decision to downsize and the strategies for implementing that decision should not be ignored. Implementation especially should reflect the enduring, operational values which the top decision makers want to govern future decisions at all levels of the organization, since this is a screaming message to the surviving employees of what really matters and what this organization really values.

The ethics of the decisions surrounding the downsizing implementation strategy are the new paradigm. They become the model. They tell all employees what the new rules are. These decisions set the standard for the ethics of future decisions.

The caution is simple, but real. Be careful what you teach your employees is ethical in this new, downsized world because they will learn it well and apply it ruthlessly. Downsizing sets the ethical standards. If it teaches that loyalty is no longer valued, don't whine that today's employees are not loyal like the employees of an earlier era. If it teaches that the ends justify the means, don't criticize employees for being shortsighted and more concerned with getting the job done than with who gets hurt along the way. If it teaches that employees are not to be trusted don't expect your employees to embrace empowerment initiatives or actively participate in employee involvement processes like Total Quality Management.

Downsizing is the critical event that demonstrates, perhaps more clearly than any other, what truly matters to you, the decision makers. It is your best chance to communicate the ethical underpinnings of the organization you are in the process of creating. Use this chance wisely. You may not get another.

Although 77% of companies saw a decline in morale after downsizing, when asked what they would do differently, executives report they would:

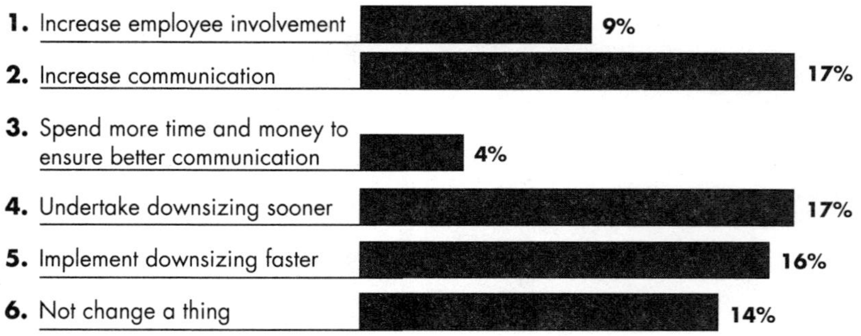

Today's employees are loyal to themselves and their profession, not to a particular organization or position. They know chances are good they will switch jobs many times; they also know that their companies can't promise lifetime contracts.

Tom Peters predicts our current reengineering efforts will fail, or at least fall short of the mark, because of the absence of trust in the workplace. Fear and distrust are still strong forces in most organizations.

Competitive organizations build high trust environments that drive their success and increase profitability. Trust means confidence—confidence that others' actions are consistent with their words, that those people with whom you work are concerned about your welfare and interests apart from what you can do for them, that the skills you have developed are respected and valued by your co-workers and the organization, and that who you are and what you believe truly matter in the workplace. Without high trust, no change effort can succeed.

Robert W. Rogers, *Executive Excellence, 7/94*

Summary Map

From Decision to Implementation

The components of downsizing

- deciding
- announcing
- implementing

Making the downsizing decision

Identify the problem:

- What is the status quo?
- What is unsatisfactory?
- What is the desired state and the alternative state?
- What will be gained by changing from the desired to the alternative states?
- Does the change create policy inconsistencies?
- Will changing the current state result in adverse legal or ethical considerations?

Identify alternatives:

- What other alternatives might be considered?
- What other alternatives does the definition of the problem allow?
- What can I do to identify solutions not yet apparent to me?

Evaluate alternatives:

- What are the likely consequences of the alternatives being considered?
- Are those alternatives acceptable?

- What will happen if we implement this alternative?
- What will it take to implement this alternative?
- How likely is it that this alternative will succeed?
- What possible negative ramifications might this alternative produce?
- What will happen if we attempt this alternative and it is not effective?
- What other information do we need before we can decide if this alternative is desirable? Optimal?
- How will we get the information we need?

Select the optimal alternative:

- How will this alternative move us closer to the desired state?
- What are the likely outcomes that will move us further away from the desired state?
- Is the net result sufficient progress towards our desired future to warrant the costs?

Implement the decision:

- How can resistance to change be minimized?
- Monitor the results.

Evaluate the decision:

- Did it work?
- Did it produce the desired result?
- Did it produce any unanticipated (desirable or undesirable) results?
- What can we learn to make the next decision better?

Implementing the decision

Form a working group responsible for implementation.

Determine how best to achieve objectives:

- Determine extent of downsizing.

- Identify positions to be eliminated.
- Identify departing employees.
- Encourage voluntary separation.
- Set time frame for process.
- Determine costs associated with decision.
- Determine what transitional benefits departing employees will receive.

Optimize the implementation decision:

- Define communication strategy.
- Determine who should be involved in implementation.
- Decide who will manage the transition.
- Decide how to define success.
- Determine how to measure the effectiveness of the implementation strategy.
- Decide how to deal with unanticipated outcomes.

Announcing the decision

Choose:

- who to tell
- what they should be told
- when the message should be delivered
- how they should be told

Employee involvement

- Co-opt resistant employees by making them part of the team that defines the implementation strategy.
- Allow employees the opportunity for personal choices for career opportunities and job continuity whenever possible.
- Don't allow morale to deteriorate.

Transition manager

Single point of contact with oversight responsibility

Manager must have:

- management's ear
- time to pay attention to the transition
- authority to sound the alarm

Chapter 3

The Evident Victims

Once the decision to downsize has been made there are a myriad of subsequent decisions facing the organization. If downsizing is the right strategic choice, then:

- What work, if any, can we afford to eliminate?
- How do we decide which people should leave the organization?
- What, if anything, are we going to do to help them through the transition?

These are the three questions we will explore as we discuss the evident victims of downsizing—those who lose their jobs.

Eliminating work

There are typically three working assumptions associated with the decision to downsize:

1. The organization will realize a strategic benefit from cutting headcount and the costs associated with that cut. (The precise nature of the anticipated benefit is usually couched in terms reflecting the dynamic between the pressures and/or opportunities in the organization's strategic environment and its current resources.)
2. We will still be able to accomplish all the critical work of the organization, even with fewer people. (The expectation is usually that there will be a combination of increased individual efficiency/productivity as well as the elimination of "noncritical" work that is currently being done.)
3. We can survive the cuts.

The first two assumptions are likely correct, at least in part. The third cannot be assumed.

The pressures to be better, faster and cheaper in today's competitive arena, to reorganize, and to get "lean and mean" in order to meet the demands of stockholders, voters, customers, regulators, *et. al.* are greater today than in any other period in recent history. There is inevitably some "fat" in the pre-downsized organization. There are bound to be inefficiencies and duplications of effort that have evolved as the organization met the prior demands of expansion and growth. It is reasonable to expect that some work can be eliminated and those resources either reallocated to more critical new tasks or eliminated from the cost of doing business.

"Most of the time, the easiest thing for companies to do is make employee cuts," says Eric Greenberg, of the AMA. "The initial bottom-line boost is addictive."

Lisa Baggerman, *Industry Week*, 1/18/93

Some form of work and resource review is unavoidable if the organization is going to cut people and eliminate work. That review can either be the driver or the consequence of the downsizing decision. Whether it is the "cart" or the "horse" doesn't change one essential fact: as we downsize we eliminate some work. How we define that work and what people are marked to leave it are based on some more or less rational approach

The worst case scenario is to use a simple financial analysis to define the size of the saving needed. Some organizations decide that they need to eliminate some predetermined dollar amount from the cost of doing business. They translate that amount into a corresponding number of organizational positions to be eliminated. That number is then calculated as a percentage of the total workforce and an across-the-board force reduction is announced, based on the same percentage of positions being cut from every organizational unit (work group, department, plant, location).

As inept as that may seem, it is not that uncommon. Rather, it is often viewed as the most attractive way of discharging an unpleasant but necessary responsibility since the decision makers at the top of the organization can claim that it is the quickest, easiest and fairest method of making the necessary cuts.

It is certainly quick and easy. No significant analysis. No systematic research. No deep thought or driving philosophical position. Just a simple formula of dollars divided by average salary plus benefits. Put a capable staff assistant in a room with an organization chart and some payroll data and the first step is done. Then announce the required cuts to the heads of the affected units and let them figure out how to implement them. Everybody is equally angry and upset, but at least it is fair.

While it does treat each unit identically, no hints of favoritism or bias here, it may be the least fair approach. It completely ignores the merits or needs of the individual units. The slothful manager who has let the organization go to fat is treated the same as the manager who has fastidiously husbanded every resource in an exercise in fiduciary responsibility.

It may also be the least strategically intelligent approach, ignoring any understanding of the long-term needs of the organization and its subsystems in favor of a simplistic attempt to spread the pain evenly.

Its attraction is that the ranking decision maker only has to justify the financial legitimacy of cutting overhead, child's play in today's environment. Lower level managers then make the specific decisions about what work to eliminate using whatever rationales they can sell up the line. Finally these managers, seeking an equally mechanical and thoughtless process for identifying who will leave, settle on some ritualistic formula such as "last in, first out" to complete the decision-making process.

What they end up with is a decision that is as bias free as it is ineffective and destructive to the organization's long-term well-being. Such decision making creates an organization where, as we will see in the following chapters, the survivors have the least to gain from recommitting to the post-downsized organization. These become the places where the survivors' desire to retaliate and their need to defend themselves from further mismanagement compete for which motive can inflict the most damage on the organization.

A more appropriate way to identify which work will be eliminated is to carefully examine the strategic requirements of the organization and rebuild it to best meet those needs. This is the process that is called such names as reengineering, rightsizing or restructuring.

This approach requires a more or less detailed review of the work that is currently being done and a determination of the work that needs to be done. This examination yields a "gap analysis" which identifies:

- work currently being done that can reasonably be eliminated
- critical work elements that need to be maintained
- new elements of work that need to be added to the current mix

The process sounds good on paper but can be suspect. It is susceptible to subtle manipulation and the influence of special interests both inside and outside the organization. Since it does not presume that "the pain will be equally shared" some units or individuals may find their positions and power enhanced by the downsizing, while others see their positions and influence nearly evaporate. The decisions as to who falls where in the new power structure can be unduly influenced if the decision recommenders or approvers are working any agenda other than the strategic well-being of the organization as a whole.

In an effort to avoid the agenda being manipulated, some organizations seek the safety of an objective third party, a consultant. There is some legitimate, potential benefit to be realized by using an outside objective source for the analysis and redesign processes. But even the most ethical consultants come to the task at hand with a set of biases and predispositions. We, for example, impose a Nadler-based diagnosis and the redefinition of mission, vision, goals and objectives on the process. We see this as a benign intervention, but it does predispose us to a solution that meets Nadler's definitions of organizational fitness.

Until recently, one of the Big Eight consulting firms had a reputation for advocating a matrix structure in nearly every organization where they were brought in to restructure, redesign or reengineer. This predisposition for a given structural model, if openly presented, is not necessarily a problem. It only becomes problematic when the consultant claims objectivity and creates the expectation that the analysis data will drive the outcome, when the likely matrix-based recommendations are masked as the result of a truly objective process.

Other consulting firms specialize in cutting the organization "to the bone". That is their belief. Cut the organization wide and deep, then rebuild with today's employees, with today's skills unencumbered by any history or expectations rooted in the pre-downsizing culture. Thus, getting rid of as many incumbent employees as possible becomes their (unspoken) goal. They are the consultants who prompted one manager to post this message to his office wall:

"The pessimist says the glass is half empty. The optimist says the glass is half full. The consultant says the glass is twice as big as we need."

No system for deciding how big a cut, or which work to cut, is foolproof or perfect. The best we can seek is a systematic and systemic analysis that is driven by strategic considerations and a genuine desire to serve the best interests of the organization and its stakeholders, and is free from the influence of preconceptions, personal ambitions or hidden agendas.

Who should leave

Nothing—not overwork, not confusion, not lost perks, not apprehension—is as deadening to a manager's morale as firing subordinates.

Lee Smith,
Fortune,
7/25/94

Several years ago a former colleague got a new job. It sounded like a dream assignment. She was going to be a special assistant to the CEO/chairman of the board of one of the biggest of the Fortune 500. We called a few months after she took on her new responsibilities and the call was answered by a woman who sounded utterly defeated.

Our former colleague's dream job had turned into a nightmare. In her case, special assistantship consisted of helping implement the strategic decision to downsize by identifying the 27,000 people whose jobs were being eliminated that year. As it turned out, a similar number of employees was to be let go over a period of five consecutive years. She was responsible for developing the processes which would be used in identifying approximately 135,000 loyal employees who were destined to become former employees as this organization redefined its mission and transformed its structures to meet that new mission. She didn't name the names. She developed the mechanism to allow others to name the names.

There are so many options for defining who will be asked or encouraged to leave. Traditionally organizations have looked for some formula that would meet two tests:

- It must be defensible, both in the courts of public opinion and law.
- It must be effective. It must produce the right results, a workable mix of employees who leave and those who remain.

Defensibility

Can the organization's actions and methods withstand the certain critical scrutiny that will surely follow the announcement of whatever scheme is employed to identify who will stay and who will go?

- Is the process legal?
- Is it consistent with all bargained for and contracted agreements governing how such decisions will be made?
- Is it consistent with the organization's stated values and how it has traditionally defined its relationship with its employees and other stakeholders?
- What will be the emotional after effects among those employees who remain? Will they see the process as fair? Intelligent? Reasonable?

Effectiveness

One critical consideration as the organization considers who will leave is the organization's future effectiveness. This is not just about dollars. It is also about skills, knowledge, wisdom, reputation and perceptions. Can the organization, given that certain work is to be eliminated, afford to lose certain people?

For example, in the hectic times immediately following the breakup of the Bell System, the newly formed regional holding companies, the "Baby Bells", were laying off employees in record numbers. One of these companies had five senior staffers who represented the total repository of knowledge regarding microwave transmission, a somewhat dated but vital technical niche. The early retirement offering was so attractive that all five of these senior technicians opted to retire. The company faced two choices: redefine the criteria for retirement to protect itself from creating gaps in its skills base that it could not afford or allow all five to leave and hope to rehire one or two as consultants.

Effectiveness concerns include:

- Are the organizational reservoirs of critical skills and knowledge being depleted?
- Can the organization afford to replenish those skills and knowledge if they are needed at some future date?
- What will be lost if certain people are no longer employed whose wisdom, insights and perspectives simply cannot be replaced in the open labor market?

- What will losing certain employees do to the organization's reputation among critical stakeholders such as stockholders, competitors and suppliers?
- What unfillable gaps will be left if the scheme identifies people the organization can ill afford to lose?
- How will exceptions to the rules of who stays and who goes, unique cases, be managed?
- Can the rules governing the layoff be changed midstream if the emerging profile of the downsized organization is not acceptable?
- What safeguards are included in the process to ensure the ongoing ability of the organization to fulfill its mission and meet its goals?

Selection mechanisms

The search goes on for the perfect selection mechanism. So far there is none. Most organizations address layoffs using some combination of the tried and true even though they are also the flawed and troublesome.

1. Seniority

This is the standby of the unions, characterized by the LIFO, Last In First Out, model. It protects those with the most years with the organization and rewards loyalty. It prevents the employer from replacing older, higher paid workers with young, less experienced workers willing to work for less.

Seniority also may include bumping rights, where a more senior employee in a job that is being eliminated can bump a more junior employee from a job that is not threatened. The formulas and specifics are usually spelled out in detail in the "working agreement" between union and management.

Among its drawbacks is that for some organizations the most junior employee population may also be the most diverse element of the employee body. A seniority-based layoff often results in the demographic profile of the organization reverting to a degree of homogeneity that may no longer be socially acceptable or responsible. Women, people of color and other diverse elements may see years of gains wiped out by strict adherence to this policy.

Many unionized organizations apply this model to their non-unionized management and professional forces as well. It provides for an internal consistency, and it is an easy, almost mindless process. It relieves management from having to make tough decisions. As an added bonus, it is very defensible. Also, because it is mindless, it is perhaps the least effective way to ensure long-term viability

2. Incumbency

This process relies on a clear statement of which positions are being eliminated. Usually a more or less detailed work analysis identifies nonessential jobs. Whoever is in those positions is laid off, irrespective of seniority, skill, knowledge or past job performance. This almost random selection process protects the mix of experience, skills, knowledge and performance. The good news is that diversity is preserved. The bad news is that the organization gets to keep a proportionate number of its least effective employees and loses an equal proportion of its best.

3. Skill sets

Some organizations endeavor to identify specific skill sets that are either critical, and thus immune from downsizing, or are no longer essential and, therefore, prime targets. Once that is done and the population narrowed, the question still remains whether seniority, incumbency or some other selection criterion should apply.

4. Job performance

There is one certainty as we discuss how to identify which employees to lay off. That is, almost no one has a sufficiently objective and defensible employee performance evaluation process as to make a purely performance-based determination of which employees are the least effective contributors to the bottom line and, thus, the most desirable to be rid of.

A purely performance-based selection process is an ideal which seems to have escaped most of us. Almost every manager dreams of being able to use the downsizing opportunity as a chance to rid the organization of weak or marginal performers and replenish the ranks with the best and brightest.

Yet between strong, seniority-based union agreements and weakly defined and poorly implemented performance measurement systems this ideal remains unattainable for most organizations. The fact remains that the system is rarely defensible. Most performance evaluation systems are a "wrongful dismissal" suit waiting to happen.

One possible exception is the officer corps of the U.S. military. In that organization "fitness" ratings drive eligibility for promotion and failure to be promoted after a predefined period of eligibility is grounds for an individual being "RIFed" (RIF being the acronym for Reduction in Forces).

5. Volunteerism

Having people volunteer to leave is one way of limiting hard feelings and fear in the post-downsized organization. Encouraging people to leave has its risks. Those who leave may wind up taking their experience, expertise and insights to a competitor. Providing incentives for people to leave can be very expensive, deferring or eliminating the short-term cost savings that downsizing is supposed to yield.

It also seems to be the most capable, the most confident and perhaps the most valuable people who choose to go. The weak, timid or uncertain are least likely to leave unless they are within just a few years of retirement and the cash incentives are too good to refuse.

6. Favoritism/nepotism

While no one will admit it, there are almost always those who have a mentor, special relationship or family member in high places who knows how to subvert the system and look out for that someone special whom they want to stay. In nearly every case we have seen, special accommodations are made for a select few. It does not matter what process is employed to identify those to be laid off, some who otherwise "qualify" for layoff survive. And their survival is due to the subtle (or not so subtle) intervention of a person with sufficient clout to bend a rule.

Managing the transition

The search for a fully effective, defensible mechanism which leaves no bitter aftertaste is, at least to date, futile. It is not unlike a recent conversation we witnessed between a nineteen-year-old college student and his father. The young man was wanting to break off a relationship with his girlfriend. Things had cooled between them and he wanted to make a clean break. He asked his father, "How do I break up with her, not hurt her feelings and not have her think I'm a real jerk?"

The answer: "You can't. No matter what you say or do, her feelings will be hurt and she will think you are a jerk. That's human nature. She'll feel hurt because she will see your decision as a personal rejection. That always hurts. If she has any self-esteem at all she will think you are a jerk, simply as a defense mechanism. After all, if you weren't a jerk you would not walk away from such a wonderful person."

No mechanism exists which "rejects" employees without leaving some residue of hurt. But some organizations continue to seek some affordable, consistent process for meeting the needs of the organization which treats departing employees in ways which are "appropriate". The problem may be that there is no agreement as to what constitutes appropriate.

Lawrence, Mittman and Greenberg, writing in *Management Review*, suggested that there are three distinct approaches to workforce reductions, three distinctly different definitions of the appropriate way to treat employees in a downsizing organization. They called these three styles:

- Preventionists
- People Pushers
- Parachute Packers

Each of these styles has its own characteristic set of processes for dealing with the need to reduce the cost of doing business.

Preventionists see downsizing as a last resort, to be avoided at nearly any cost. It may be the least desirable alternative for achieving lasting cost-cutting goals since, rather than reduce headcount, they prefer strategies like hiring freezes, job sharing, shortened work days or work weeks and part-time employment.

If payroll must be cut, Preventionists advocate wage and salary rollbacks. Preventionists seem to hope that the necessity for cuts is temporary and the storm can be weathered if we all stick together. This style then avoids layoffs. It reshapes how work is done and if some work is eliminated, it is done without requiring either temporary or permanent layoffs.

People Pushers seek to use voluntary means to reduce workforce. They offer incentives for people selecting early retirements and voluntary separations. They can avoid making people leave if only they can attract enough volunteers in addition to the natural reductions in force resulting from routine attrition. To help prepare employees to leave they are also advocates of liberal transfer policies and employee retraining. So here the selection process is voluntary and therefore, some would suppose, least likely to result in negative impacts on motivation and morale.

Boeing tries to cushion the blow of layoffs by providing extensive out-placement operations to help the employee find another job. The company provides free counseling services, help in preparing resumes, and coaching in interview skills, along with use of long-distance phones and fax machines. Our main job is to facilitate face-to-face communications, for there's no better way to create a feeling of community.

Michael J. Major,
Public Relations Journal,
12/93

Parachute Packers just go ahead and lay people off if that is what they think the organization needs. Paradoxically, even though the layoff may be economically motivated, Parachute Packers provide some of the most generous separation allowances and economic benefits, the golden parachutes or golden handshakes we hear so much about.

The authors also make brief reference to two other types which define the extremes of the scales. Purgers simply cut people loose, letting them make their own way in the job market with nothing more than a "thank you," if that. Perfectionists do everything within their power first to prevent or delay layoffs and then, when the layoff is inevitable, to provide for the well-being of those who are leaving.

The idea of clearly defined and distinct downsizing styles is appealing in making the complex and difficult appear easier to comprehend, but may be off the mark. Rather than three or five distinct types, we are seeing a continuum ranging from the layoff, uncushioned by any special benefits or subsidies at one extreme, to the incented, subsidized, voluntary outplacement at the other.

Nowhere in our experience have we seen the clean-cut examples that the authors suggest. Nearly every employer utilizes a hybrid style. They may be Preventionists or Parachute Packers with their executives, People Pushers or Perfectionists with their middle management and Purgers with front-line employees.

The authors' further suggestion that there is a predictable relationship between the type and size of the organization, its segment in the market (manufacturing, service, government) or the level/position of the employees seems to lack predictive value. The typology may be useful for describing a given organization at a given time, but we are observing a migration through a variety of combinations and permutations of these styles in organizations as they cycle through successive layoffs.

Take public utilities as an example. According to the authors, regulated utilities are the "prototypical people pushers". For generations they sought to prevent layoffs. They pushed people out with generous retirement offers as economic need demanded downsizing. But they also laid off thousands, with impunity, as the volunteer base dried up and further cuts were still called for.

The point that seems to have been missed was that layoffs recur. They are not a one-time phenomenon. As one electric company employee put it following two successive layoffs in three years in a company that had not laid off anyone for 75 years: "The first time was culture shock. Laying off loyal employees was painful. After the first layoff, it got surprisingly easier. I expect that downsizing will become just another management tool in the future."

This suggests that at least some Preventionists, People Pushers and Parachute Packers learn how to lay off people less compassionately, over time. This suggests that there may be a corollary argument to that which claims that violence in films and on TV numbs us to real-life violence. Perhaps successive layoffs numb the decision makers to the individual hurt caused by the decision. And perhaps that distancing from the pain is a psychological necessity if we are going to continue to ask mere mortals to make decisions that benefit one class of organizational stakeholders at so dear a cost to another class of stakeholders.

As for Lawrence, Mittman and Greenberg's conclusions, their data and analysis make fascinating reading and may be useful in suggesting available alternatives, but we would be reluctant to recommend their model as an alternative to a strategic analysis.

The most consistent indicator of how to manage the transition of employees from active to inactive status seems to be strategic, rather than stylistic. The operative questions should be:

- What are we trying to accomplish through this layoff?
- What are the costs and benefits of the various options?
- Which set of costs and benefits yields the most of what we are trying to accomplish at a cost which we are willing to pay?

Key to this analysis is long-term strategic thinking and recognizing all the costs, not just those that are apparent to the beancounters. Part of that strategic view is to keep the objectives of the decision in sight.

Objectives may include:

- eliminating some given number of employees, or a given number of dollars, from the payroll as a means of driving down operating costs
- introducing a new structure which facilitates the more efficient or effective realization of strategic goals
- adopting new technologies to enhance efficiency, effectiveness and service quality
- maintaining the reputation as a desirable employer in order to facilitate employee recruitment and/or retention
- expanding into new markets or lines of business which call for a different distribution of skills and competencies
- exiting existing markets
- maintaining the support of a given strategic stakeholder by attending to their particular agenda
- demonstrating (living by) a given set of values or beliefs regarding how organizations should conduct themselves
- moving the organization nearer to some driving strategic vision of the future

Costs include:

- dollars spent in diagnosis, analysis and the development of a lay-off strategy
- potential loss of employee commitment from those who survive the downsizing
- time lost to formal and informal discussions of the state of the organization, its managers and the impact of downsizing-related decisions
- dollars needed to retrain employees to prepare them for new tasks and new technologies
- damage to the reputations of the organization and its leadership
- loss of key stakeholder support
- potential legal claims of wrongful dismissal, discrimination or other lay-off related issues
- dollars spent for separation allowances, enhanced retirements and accelerated or enhanced benefits packages to those who leave, either voluntarily or involuntarily
- loss of trust as past promises are violated and the truth is seen to be sacrificed in favor of expediency

Obviously, neither of these is an all-inclusive list. The task for the organizational decision makers is to create an expansive list of all conceivable strategic objectives and their associated tangible and intangible costs. The greatest risk and the most likely cause of an ineffective or inappropriate choice regarding what work to eliminate, which people should leave the organization and what, if anything, to do to help them through the transition is the use of too narrowly defined a set of strategic goals and costs of implementation.

Conclusion

The lesson for the future may be that, after the dust settles, one priority for every organization which sees the likelihood of future downsizing should be the development and implementation of a manageable and defensible performance evaluation system. Every organization stands to benefit from adopting some workable process for the ongoing identification and development or removal of its poorest performers.

Naturally, such a system should be fair, based on a premise that every employee deserves clear expectations, effective feedback, adequate training and ample opportunity to learn, with ongoing coaching and counseling. But proven nonperformers should not be tolerated. That is one way that we can right some of the inequities and inefficiencies of the current systems which seem to force organizations to lay off some of their most valued employees while retaining some whose contribution to the organization's goals and objectives is marginal at best.

In the following chapters we go into greater detail on some of the unanticipated costs facing most organizations as they elect to downsize. We discuss the issues facing employees, supervisors/managers and executives and the costs of both ignoring and dealing with them.

To overcome myopia, we need to re-educate, redesign, and change administrative policies and programs to support new initiatives. Do you suffer from myopia? If your answers to the following questions are negative, you probably suffer from functional myopia and have some work to do.

- *Have all company business processes been charted and analyzed?*
- *Do all employees understand the company's basic value chain and how their work fits into that chain?*
- *Is cross-functional teamwork common practice?*
- *Are employees measured not only by functional goals and standards, but also by how much they contribute to the overall success of the company?*
- *Do administrative policies and procedures encourage a wide view of the company's business?*

Daniel R. Tobin, *Executive Excellence*, 8/94

Summary Map

The Evident Victims

Eliminating work

Assumptions:

- The organization will realize strategic benefit from cutting costs.
- The organization will be able to accomplish all critical, required work.
- The organization can survive the cuts.

Identifying work to be eliminated

Examine the organization's strategic requirements.

Examine "gap analysis" to identify:

- work that can be eliminated
- work that must be maintained
- work that needs to be added to the mix

Use an objective third party (consultant) to avoid manipulation of gap analysis data by special interests.

Formula for determining who should leave

- must be defensible in eyes of public and under law
- must produce the right results

Defensibility of formula for determining who will leave

- Is the process legal?

- Is it consistent with bargained agreements that govern such actions?
- Is it consistent with the organization's stated values?

Maintaining effectiveness during downsizing

- Will critical skills and knowledge be depleted?
- Can essential skills and knowledge be replenished if needed?
- What special knowledge will be lost if individuals critical to the organization leave?
- How will exceptions to the rules of who stays and goes be managed?
- Can the rules be changed if it appears the results are unacceptable?
- What safeguards ensure ongoing mission fulfillment?

Downsizing selection mechanisms

Seniority:

- LIFO—Last In, First Out
- Rewards longevity
- May include bumping rights
- May cause diversity imbalance
- Least effective way to ensure long-term viability

Incumbency:

- Based on work analysis
- Dictates that people in positions scheduled for elimination leave regardless of seniority or ability
- Diversity preserved
- Some of the least effective employees may be retained.

Skill Sets:

- Identify specific skill sets immune from downsizing.

- Narrow population to those matching skill set and then apply other downsizing criteria.

Job performance:

- Most performance evaluations are not purely performance-based.
- Most are "wrongful dismissal" suits waiting to happen.

Volunteerism:

- Providing incentives to leave can be expensive.
- Frequently, the best and most valuable people are the ones who choose to go.

Favoritism/Nepotism:

- Special accommodations are made for a select few.
- Usually happens when a mentor with sufficient clout bends a rule.

Managing the transition

No mechanism exists which will prevent departing employees from feeling hurt

Styles of dealing with downsizing according to a *Management Review* article:

- Preventionists who see downsizing as a last resort to be avoided at nearly any cost
- People Pushers who seek to use voluntary means to reduce force
- Parachute Packers who just go ahead and lay off people if that is what they feel the organization needs
- Purgers who cut people loose with nothing more than a "thank you" (an extreme)
- Perfectionists who do everything possible to prevent layoffs and then do everything possible to see to the well-being of employees when layoffs become inevitable (the other extreme)

Almost all employers follow styles which are hybrids of those just discussed, combining styles depending on the employee levels involved.

Questions to ask when managing the downsizing effort:

- What are we trying to accomplish?
- What are the costs and benefits of the various options?
- Which set of costs and benefits yields the most of what we are trying to accomplish at a cost which we are willing to pay?

Potential downsizing objectives

- driving down operating costs
- introducing new structure to meet strategic goals
- adopting new technologies
- maintaining a reputation as a desirable employer
- expanding into new markets or lines of business
- exiting existing markets
- maintaining the support of stakeholders
- demonstrating a given set of values
- moving the organization closer to a strategic vision

Potential costs

- dollars spent for diagnosis and strategy development
- potential loss of employee commitment from survivors of downsizing
- time lost discussing the state of the business
- retraining dollars
- damage to the reputations of the organization and the leadership
- loss of key stakeholder support
- potential legal claims for wrongful dismissal or other perceived wrongs
- dollars spent for separation allowances
- loss of trust as past promises are violated

Chapter 4

The Other Victims

In the preceding chapter we discussed the *evident* victims of downsizing, those who lose their jobs through the process. Here we will expand the definition of who is a victim to include those who survive downsizing. Our concern for those who remain in the downsizing organization will focus on three classes of employees:

- front-line employees
- their supervisors/managers
- executives

We will identify a number of issues facing each class of survivor, setting the stage for the following chapters which address the "what-to's" and "how-to's" of caring for these survivors of downsizing.

Front-line employees

From this perspective there are several critical issues that need to be addressed if these employees are to become optimally productive contributors to the newly downsized organization.

- grieving
- resistance to change
- fear
- distrust
- increasing workload

- developing new skills
- decreasing systems support
- deciding to recommit

Grieving

In her book, *On Death and Dying*, Elisabeth Kübler-Ross described the reactions people commonly experience when facing terminal illness or the death of a loved one. The grieving process, as it has come to be called, is not unique to times relating to death or illness. We see the same sequence of reactions among those who are employed by an organization undergoing significant changes, including downsizing. The employees' stages of grieving, adapted from Kübler-Ross' work, are:

- denial
- anger
- blame (others)
- guilt (self-blame)
- adaptation/accommodation

By the time they reach the status of survivor, most employees are beyond denial, although some employees never move beyond denial. As recently as 1992 a few employees of the former Bell System were still telling anyone within earshot that the 1984 breakup of their former organization into regional companies had been a mistake and that "they" (the government) would realize it soon and put the System back together.

But for most, the reality of downsizing is a wake-up call that moves them beyond denial into the later stages of the grieving process. Downsizing becomes an undeniable reality. Depending on individual circumstances and psychology the employee may pass readily through the remaining stages to adaptation/ accommodation or may get stuck.

The first sticking place is anger. People in this stage have not moved far from denial. They are still struggling with sentiments such as, "This isn't fair. This isn't right." They accept that the event has happened but are still dealing with it from a purely emotional perspective. Anger is such a strong polarizing force that it truly blinds these employees from seeing any potential for good in the decision to downsize. To maintain their anger they block out rational arguments supporting that which they are choosing to rail against. Their anger, at this stage, is fierce and generally unfocused.

The next sticking place is blame. These employees are now directing their anger at those they hold responsible for the events leading up to the decision to downsize. They expend their energies identifying who should be held accountable and dreaming up appropriate ways of dealing with these people of power.

The final stage where people get stuck is guilt. In this context one can argue that guilt is anger directed at the self rather than others. Guilt, like anger, takes two distinct forms following downsizing: guilt about the decision and guilt about the consequences.

Companies devote vast resources to dealing with the trauma of downsizing, but most of that goes to the most obvious victims—those let go.

Lee Smith,
Fortune,
7/25/94

Decision guilt sounds like, "If only I/we had . . ." This form of guilt stems from the belief that if the employee(s) had acted differently the decision to downsize might not have been necessary. For example:

- if only we had worked harder
- if only we had not struck for higher wages
- if only we had been more flexible about work rules

Consequence-oriented guilt follows from employees comparing their situations with those of their fellows who are no longer employed. Here they judge their worth and question the fairness or the circumstances which allowed them to survive when others did not. This is especially likely to become a sticking point if the employees who were released are now in difficult straits. The single parent who goes from full employment with benefits to welfare status may become an object of pity. Guilt about that person's hardships becomes even more likely when the surviving employee is financially secure, when they are a second income earner in a family or when they view themselves as less deserving of the job than their less fortunate former comrade.

Survivor guilt is compounded when the survivor experiences positive feelings ranging from relief to joy at having escaped the terrible fate that has befallen others, often followed by a sense of shame for having felt that way.

Survivor guilt, especially when it is consequence oriented, is a well documented phenomenon. Usually associated with war, train wrecks and natural disasters, it applies to the man-made disaster of downsizing as well.

The important lesson is that guilt is real, can be debilitating and will not necessarily go away by itself. While time may heal all wounds, it can also leave scars. Those scars may prevent the full reintegration of the guilty employee back into the effective workforce.

Resistance to change

A second issue for employees is that downsizing is, if nothing else, a change. Many employees resist change even when their employment status is not threatened. When that threat is present it is not at all surprising to find even more resistance than might be otherwise expected.

Resistance is another of those phenomena that has been widely explored and is reasonably well understood. It stems from a variety of sources, several of which (fear, distrust, the need to master new skills) are detailed below.

Resistance to the changes associated with downsizing is compounded by its sheer size and scope. It is the multiplicity of concurrent changes that we associate with downsizing which expands and deepens the level of resistance employees demonstrate. It is important to recognize that the earlier lessons learned about reducing resistance to change may not work in the aftermath of downsizing. While the resistance is fundamentally the same as in other, less traumatic situations, the depth of the resistance may render it immune to the usual interventions.

Fear

Resistance to change is often associated with fear. You might ask what survivors have to be afraid of. After all, they have managed to keep their jobs.

Downsizing stirs up primal fears in every employee. Going back to Maslow's *Hierarchy of Needs* we learned that survival is primary, and what is more essential to survival in today's society than having a job? Being employed is not only tied to our ability to provide food and shelter to our families. It is also tied to our sense of being accepted by others and our sense of self.

Finding yourself suddenly (and involuntarily) unemployed stirs up all sorts of uncertainties. But you don't have to be separated from the organization to experience that gut wrenching base fear. It is sufficient to be associated with the process. There is a residual effect from a downsizing which affects everybody in the organization.

By and large, survivors progress through three stages after a layoff:

- *a sense of anguish*
- *a neutral stage*
- *a time when survivors get a grip on themselves and become productive employees again*

Warren Boroson and Linda Burgess, *Across the Board,* 11/92

First among the fears is that downsizing once begun will become an ongoing process and though you may have survived this round, there is bound to be another and you may not be so lucky the second time around. One survivor characterized that perspective this way, "Once the sharks have tasted the blood, they'll be back for more." For many, a first downsizing is a signal of more to come, just as a first shark reaching a disabled swimmer is the signal for an uncontrolled feeding frenzy.

Once the expectation of secure employment has been violated, the fear creeps into each employee's consciousness and continues to eat away at confidence, motivation, trust, commitment, self-esteem and all the rest. This nascent fear is magnified when the employee has to work to higher standards, with increased workloads or on new and different tasks.

Distrust

For employees entering the workforce in the fifties, sixties, and seventies there was a commonly held assumption about the social contract of work. Young men and women seeking their first jobs had been led to believe that employment was a right and that anyone willing to abide by a few simple rules could be confident of continuing employment. There were no written contracts that guaranteed lifetime employment, but there was a social contract of sorts. With the exception of a few well defined industries which hired and laid off large numbers of employees in cycles dictated by large scale contracts, such as aerospace and defense, continuing employment was conditional on three things:

- doing what you were told
- staying out of trouble
- meeting the performance minimums

The other set of assumptions was based on an interesting paradox. On one hand employees placed their blind trust in the organization's leadership. They chose to act as though they believed that their leaders knew what they were doing. They acted as if leaders knew and understood what was necessary for the organization's long-term viability and would not risk that viability out of shortsightedness or greed. At the same time they were vocal about their disdain for these same leaders and decisions that reflected poor judgment or lack of concern for key stakeholders.

Most big firms may never achieve the gains that are supposed to justify such wrenching changes.

That is because they are tearing up the implicit contract they have always had with managers and other professionals: security of long-term employment in exchange for dogged loyalty. David Nadler, an American management consultant, says, "The problem is that many companies have given no indication of what the new psychological contract is."

The Economist, 4/3/93

In their naïveté, employees discounted what they saw with their own eyes and stuck to the myth that all would be well. As we have learned since, denial is the first response to unwanted change so it should not be surprising that employees, in large numbers, chose to trust their existence to the very leaders they disparaged.

Unfortunately, most leaders did nothing to encourage employees to take more responsibility for the success of the organization and the eventual viability of their employment. Those who tried often found themselves facing powerful lobbies, including unions, which found it to their advantage to perpetuate the myth of lifetime employment as an enforceable social contract.

So employees stuck to a simple set of beliefs with the hope that abiding by the three rules of the social contract of work was tantamount to a guarantee of lifetime employment.

Downsizing which results in employees who followed the rules losing their jobs undermines employee's trust of the organization and its leaders. If trust is the residue of promises fulfilled, then downsizing, which violates an implied promise of continuing employment, is sufficient grounds for distrust.

What compounds the distrust and extends it beyond the organization to its leaders is that in most cases the communication of anticipated events and the motives which underlie them is less than candid and accurate. Employees believe that senior leaders are scapegoating, dismissing employees to correct their own mistakes: ineffective planning, overstaffing, poor marketing decisions resulting in reduced market share or declining

declining growth, overdependence on technology, and perhaps most important, not caring about the needs of employees and their families.

Finally, distrust is amplified when the price being paid for what is seen as ineffective leadership is not being borne proportionally by all levels of the organization. If leaders are seen as prospering in hard times while employees are called upon to make increasing sacrifices, the sense of fair play is violated and trust diminished. One key indicator of fairness is salary treatment. Executive bonuses do not go down well with employees who are surviving downsizing.

Downsizing can create a climate of fear and anxiety for the remaining employees. When this is combined with increased workloads because of fewer employees, absenteeism and turnover can increase. The end result is a less-for-less net sum.

Arthur G. Davis,
Paper, Film & Foil Converter,
6/94

Consider the film *Roger and Me*. This was a dramatic expression of the perceived unfairness of Roger Smith, General Motors' chairman, who prospered amidst plant closings, unemployment and hardship. The film makers directly attributed GM's problems to Smith's inept management. Smith, symbolic of all GM management, was the focus for the accusations of unfairness. It is interesting that the perceived unfairness became a bigger issue than the management ineptitude.

Contrast GM with Chrysler. Whether you are a fan of his or not, Lee Iacocca earned high marks for his salary posture when he took over a failing Chrysler Corporation. He took a nominal salary of one dollar plus a ton of Chrysler stock, pinning his financial rewards to his success in reviving the organization. Employees believed that to be fair. That gesture went a long way towards earning much needed trust and employee support.

Increasing workload

As we have discussed above, one of the underlying premises behind many downsizing strategies is the expectation that the organization can learn to do more with less. It is the front-line employees who are ultimately expected to do more. They view the scenario differently. Rather than doing more *with less*, they see it as doing more *for less*. One nearly universal cry is that "I am being required to do more work for less money."

That workload increases as organizations downsize is not disputed by any of those we interviewed. And it increases two ways.

Some employees are being asked to do more of the work they have always done. For example if one person in a group of nine leaves, the strategy may be to redistribute the work among the remaining eight employees, rather than backfill the position. Now every employee has nine hours of work to do in their eight hour shift. Management's assumption may be that there are efficiencies to be realized. Employees often assume that doing the extra work is an invitation for management to continue this strategy until the workload is overwhelming and the employees eventually fail, motivating management to finally seek alternative means of accomplishing the work at hand.

Developing new skills

The second way work increases is for management to expand the definition of the individual's job. Now the employee may have more hours of work to do compounded by having to perform work that requires them to acquire new knowledge, master new skills and establish new relationships. These demands are further threats to the self-confidence of many employees, who fear that if they fail in these new tasks their job is at even greater risk.

Having to learn new tasks puts employees at risk in two ways. On one hand they are concerned that they may not be able to master the new skills and they therefore feel vulnerable. They also lose whatever preeminent status they may have enjoyed as masters of the task as it was done before. Learning a new task puts them at the same level as everyone else, so there is a loss of position within the group for those employees who were "past masters" of the work.

Decreasing systems support

The first decrease in support comes from initially "targeting" jobs that are viewed as "nice to have" but not "essential" such as staff support. The very experts who resided in organizational staffs are often among the first to be eliminated. Now there is no one to provide training in new skills, no subject matter experts to fill in knowledge gaps and no one with whom to establish mutually supporting relationships for those employees having to master new tasks.

The "less" in "doing more with less" goes beyond headcount. Decreasing systems support typically includes decreasing budgets. Downsizing is part of a larger cost savings strategy that rarely starts and stops with people. Employees are finding that there is less money for materials, supplies, technology and resources. They cannot go out and buy what they need to do the job. Capital and discretionary budgets are being squeezed ever more tightly.

The diminishing store of resources makes the task of doing more with less even more daunting. From the employees' perspective they face more work, new work, smaller budgets and less help.

The last, and often overlooked, form of diminishing support is the immediate supervisor him/herself. Very often, right along with downsizing, we see expanded spans of control. Supervisors are facing the same requirement that they do more with less. They have less time for each employee. Less time to provide direction, information, encouragement, support, training, feedback and all of the other essentials for employees under increasing demands.

The recommitment program begins when the downsizing is initially planned and is affected by issues that relate directly to the laid-off employees. Many messages are communicated to all employees through the separation process—the way separated employees are notified, the benefits they receive and the security procedures that are instituted after the separation. This either can communicate stability or uncertainty.

Lewis Kravitz,
Business Altanta,
12/93

Deciding to recommit

The final issue we will discuss from the perspective of the front-line employee is the choice of commitment. For many employees whether or not to care about the organization is a natural question, given that the organization and its leaders are often viewed as having betrayed the employee body in general and the individual survivor in particular.

The organizational assumption of employee loyalty is called into question early in the post-downsizing experience. Employees are asked to accept added responsibility, added work load, decreased resources and sometimes decreasing pay. Opportunities for advancement and growth are often diminished. The very motivators that drive positive employee behaviors under normal conditions are no longer promised in time of uncertainty.

To automatically expect employee commitment to organizational goals and objectives, to service and product quality standards and even to the continuing viability of the organization itself may be naïve. Employees need the opportunity to consider if, and under what circumstances, they are willing to recommit to an organization which in their minds may have already irreparably betrayed a previous trust.

The issue of employee commitment is ultimately going to hinge on their perception of two things:

- Did leadership act fairly?
- Is leadership being responsive to their post-downsizing needs?

These issues are discussed below.

Supervisors/Managers

Front-line supervisors and managers, those who oversee the day-to-day operations of the employees discussed above, may be the key employees in the organization's survival effort. Their success will be determined by how effectively they deal with the two sets of issues they face.

First of all it is important to remember that they are not just supervisors and managers. They are also employees of a downsizing organization. As such they are survivors no less than those they supervise. Every issue described above, facing individual employees, is an issue they have to face personally. All of the concerns regarding grieving, fear, trust, increasing workload, decreasing support, new skills and the decision regarding commitment apply to these people as well.

Plus, they have the added burden of dealing with five additional issues inherent in their roles as supervisors and managers:

- diffusing grief and resistance in the employees they oversee
- supporting an unpopular decision
- raising expectations while reducing support
- balancing accountability and authority
- transitioning their employees and themselves into new roles

1. Diffusing grief and resistance in the employees they oversee

Reality dictates that front-line supervisors aid and facilitate their employees' movement through the five stages of grieving. Unless and until they recognize the pain their employees are experiencing and accept an appropriate degree of responsibility for providing support and comfort, their ability to accomplish the task at hand, especially in light of the resource pressures, will be severely hampered.

They must also face the resistance to this and future changes that their employees are apt to express.

Grieving and resistance are predictable responses to any major organizational change. They are not unique to downsizing. Experienced supervisors have encountered these issues in the past and many can confidently and successfully address them if they dedicate the appropriate time and energy to the task. They should be forewarned, however, that the issues are more complex and more resistant to easy resolution in organizations undergoing downsizing than in other more routine change environments. They must also recognize the added stresses and strains they face as their jobs are changing and realize that meeting the needs of their employees will severely stretch the limits of their own emotional and psychological resources.

John Parkington, of Wyatt & Co., says "The definition of 'reasonable' is shifting. Managers are accepting tougher demands as a way of life."

Anne B. Fisher,
Fortune,
11/30/92

2. Supporting an unpopular decision

Front-line supervisors and managers are walking a tightrope when it comes to the fundamental management strategy enacted by the organization. They most likely were not party to the decision to reduce headcount, limit resources, reorganize, restructure and otherwise change how business is done. Nor are they necessarily pleased with the decision and convinced that it was the best choice, given the circumstances.

Yet they are representatives of management and as such have an obligation to represent management to their employees. One manager described his direct reporting supervisors as "transparent" to the organization. They acted as conduits for management decisions, but when questioned by their employees about the decision were quick to pass the responsibility for unpopular choices along to their higher management. If there was good news they were quick to take credit. If there was bad news they were equally quick to blame "them" for it. They betrayed the trust placed in them by the organization by refusing to support the difficult decisions which senior management deemed necessary.

In part this may be because they lacked information as to the merits of the decision. It may be that they felt inappropriately excluded from the decision-making process. Perhaps no one asked them how to best resolve the problem. Or it may simply be that they were more concerned with the acceptance of those they supervise than with their obligation to the organization. Whatever the motive, transparent behavior is ineffective.

Ultimately it disempowers those who use it. It confirms the belief that supervisors and managers are powerless. It also supports the perception that they add little value to the organization and can be removed from the organizational hierarchy with few consequences.

Supervisors and managers must find ways to support the downsizing decision if they are to be effective in managing within the environment it creates. Joining their employees in a "pity party", crying together in their collective beer, may form a short-term bond based on the *misery loves company* effect, but it is no basis from which to supervise or manage a workforce.

3. Raising expectations while reducing support (doing more with less)

Another challenge facing the line supervisor/manager is that the same external forces which dictated a cost-reduction strategy will typically cause the organization to renew its emphasis on increased productivity. Performance standards tend to increase concurrently with reductions in headcount and budget. There is a perverse logic at work here. Downsizing is a response to market pressures. Those pressures demand that costs decline while the attractiveness of the product or service increases through innovation and continuous quality improvements. Management, therefore, finds itself raising the performance standards in the midst of cutting resources.

This "double whammy" confuses and angers employees. They do not see the logic in expecting them to work to higher standards, under increased pressures where there is no apparent benefit to them. The argument that the benefit is that they get to keep their jobs has worn thin. Like the boy who cried wolf, the cry of organizational poverty and the benefit of continuing employment fail to arouse much of a response among today's employees. They are embittered by years of decreases in their purchasing power and standard of living. They are frustrated that they cannot continue to look forward to pay raises and promotions. They are frightened that their livelihood is no longer under their control.

The challenge facing the supervisor is to find ways to represent management's decisions to raise standards and decrease resources so that employees will accept today's realities and move forward. They must also represent the legitimate needs of their employees for the resources and support necessary to accomplish the task at hand. To do this they need credibility in both quarters.

The supervisor needs to be a trusted bridge between front-line employees and upper management who carries communication in both directions and effectively represents two constituencies to each other. This is an underappreciated and increasingly difficult task for which too many front-line supervisors and managers are inadequately prepared.

4. Balancing accountability and authority

Along with downsizing many organizations are redefining the locus of accountability and authority. The move towards empowering employees places another demand on the supervisor/manager. It is a truism that one can delegate authority but cannot delegate responsibility. As a supervisor you are responsible for the effective accomplishment of the assigned work. If you choose to allow certain employees added authority to act independently you may do so, but you do it at your own peril. You will be held accountable for the results. If the employee fails, it is your judgment to allow him/her that freedom which will come back to haunt you.

In the midst of downsizing many organizations are choosing empowerment as a strategy to allow for expanded workloads and spans of control. They have bought into the belief that empowering employees creates the capacity for doing more with less. Unfortunately, too many empowering efforts are poorly conceived and dismally executed. The failures of the empowering strategy outnumber the successes.

Failure is often the result of adopting an attractive philosophy without understanding what it entails and without an implementation strategy that promises a high likelihood of success. Empowering employees becomes the *programme du jour,* just another passing management fad. When empowering succeeds its results are enviable. It succeeds, in part, when supervisors and managers learn how to balance authority and accountability.

One of the first things to go as the flame flickers is creative spirit.

Lee Smith, *Fortune,* 7/25/94

Supervisors who understand empowering employees as a process know that they retain accountability for their decisions but must also hold those whom they have empowered accountable as well. They understand that they have the authority to empower and that there are criteria for determining to whom and when. They further understand that empowering others requires a degree of letting go of traditional individual power in exchange for a new, collective power where each party to the action accepts the authority and accountability commensurate with their role in the specific situation at hand. It is this challenge which faces supervisors in a downsizing environment, as they must balance which power to retain and which to share, which accountabilities to retain and which to impose on others.

5. Transitioning their employees and themselves into new roles

Midlevel bosses face two incompatible assignments: be a cold-blooded cost cutter, and be liked. Notes the Menninger Clinic's Dr. Rosen: he has been told that the new management style of the nineties is to think of himself and his people as teammates. But in front of his subordinates the manager has to play contradictory roles: he is their friend; he may also be their executioner.

Lee Smith, *Fortune*, 7/25/94

The final challenge we will discuss here concerns the transition into new roles. As suggested above, front-line employees are being asked to accept additional responsibility for doing what heretofore has been "management work". Supervisors and managers are being asked to forfeit the roles of subject matter expert and authority figure and replace them with the roles of coach, mentor, partner.

For the supervisor this requires that self-worth and perceived worth to others be divorced from the traditional behaviors of coordination, command and control. Supervisors can only make this transition if they are competent, confident and motivated.

Competence presumes that they know what new skills and knowledge these roles require and that they are given the opportunity to develop them sufficiently. Confidence stems from the belief that one can perform the tasks required at the level needed to be successful. Motivation results from knowing what is necessary, believing that one can do it, and both understanding and valuing the consequences associated with success.

The biggest unknown facing supervisors and managers in a downsizing organization is in the area of consequences. These key people must believe that the organization values them and will provide rewards for the successful accomplishment of the difficult tasks they face. At this point, the front-line supervisors and managers look to the executive level of the organization for clues as to what the future may hold. They evaluate the probabilities that they will receive their due and make their decisions accordingly. The ultimate key to organizational success remains, as it always has, in the hands of its leaders. No matter how competent and dedicated the employees and their line management, the future success of the organization is in the hands of the few, those who pilot the organizational ship through society's turbulent waters.

Executives

As with employees and supervisors/managers, there are several issues facing this population. We will deal with five:

- focusing on the strategy
- facing reality vs. preserving myths
- making the productivity promise come true
- rebuilding trust, confidence and commitment
- downsizing redux

1. Focusing on the strategy

It is the executives' responsibility to pilot the organization through uncharted waters and that means keeping their eyes on the world outside the organization. Day-to-day running of the organization must be left to line management. It is line management who are the tacticians who, given the mission, decide how best to get it done. Executives are charged with defining that mission and preparing the organization to meet it.

David Nadler takes a "systems" look at the role of executives through his Organization Performance Model. He suggests that executives are charged with attending to the organization's environment, resources and history. Their task then becomes formulating an organizational purpose (mission, vision and values), setting long-term goals and outlining broad actions needed for success.

In the downsizing environment executives must be strategically astute. Downsizing must be the right response to environmental pressures imposed by competition, suppliers, customers, regulators, labor pools and the influences of other key stakeholders, not just a trendy response to economic pressures. Executives must be attuned to the tangible and intangible resources available to the organization and must consider how best to allocate those resources in meeting the demands of the environment. They must also be students of the organization's culture, understanding its unique personality, so that they might predict how the organization will deal with subtle or not-so-subtle changes in direction.

By remaining focused on the strategy executives live up to their responsibility for honest stewardship of the organization. They can claim, and deserve, the trust of all constituencies, including employees and front-line supervisors/managers.

2. Facing reality vs. preserving myths

Part of the strategic focus is the ability to differentiate between what we know and what we think we know. Especially in the "history" component of the strategic model described above, it is critical to distinguish between reality and wishful thinking.

For example, some organizations have a self-deluding perception of their degree of invulnerability. If they see themselves as somehow assured a position of prominence in their particular realm they may develop an arrogance which can ultimately blind them to reality, leading to disastrous strategic errors. We can see this in those organizations which have misread their significance and paid too much heed to their own rhetoric.

One classic example in recent US history was PATCO, the Professional Air Traffic Controllers Organization. Early in the Reagan presidency they misread their strategic importance and struck, holding the nation's airlines hostage to their demands. In a matter of weeks PATCO was disemboweled by an unsympathetic government.

Failure to differentiate between myth and reality is a strategic error of magnum proportion. With downsizing it is crucial to read the culture of the organization accurately so that the strategic decision to downsize will yield the promised results. Misreading the culture and norms of the organization leads to unrealistic expectations, unfulfillable promises and unanticipated changes in direction. These errors in judgment can result in the destruction of executive credibility in the boardroom and on the shop floor.

One potentially destructive myth is the promise of doing more with less. This myth has been around since Henry Ford's first assembly line and the advent of Taylor's "Scientific Management" school which spawned our first management consultants, the efficiency experts.

In more recent times the myth has been kept alive as the fundamental promise justifying investments in emerging technologies. One of the Bell operating companies explored this myth in the mid 1980s. An operational vice-president asked his staff to review the proposals for investment in computer systems covering the past ten years. In every case the argument for the system included a promise of how many people the system would save. They concluded that if all of those promises had been fulfilled, every employee of that company would have been "saved" 1.3 times.

Yet it is that very promise which convinces many organizations to downsize.

The final myth, and perhaps the most potentially destructive, is that downsizing is a strategy of last resort, that it is what a failing organization clings to as a last hope.

Reality is that downsizing is a strategic choice that is just as appropriate and opportune in times of organizational success, high profit and growth as it appears to be in times of despair and desperation.

If the promise of lifetime employment is not the operative mechanism for earning employee loyalty then the role of the organization as a provider of employment is not the core mission.

Organizations exist to serve a purpose in society, to meet a need. They have a mission, vision and set of values that are defined by the opportunities and constraints present in their environment. Rarely is that mission defined as "to provide employment". The notable exception was the depression-era social programs which did have as their mission the creation of jobs.

For most organizations and, hence, their executives, the reality is that employment is a side effect. Their core mission is to do the work that society demands, to serve the designated customers and to do so in a way that allows the organization to meet its strategic goals. Maintaining a given employee population size is rarely a strategic goal. Nor should it be.

The myth that the organization exists to provide employees with jobs can lead decision makers to postpone downsizing when it is the right response for the time. The myth that profitable organizations cannot or should not downsize, that to do so is immoral or unconscionable, is wrong. Just as is it wrong to assume that it is somehow unethical for executives to be rewarded with salary increases and bonuses for better management when that better management includes the elimination of unnecessary positions, levels or functions.

A survey last year of over 1,200 executives and managers by Right Associates, an outplacement firm, found that while survivors are likely to be told about the effects of a downsizing, little may be done to introduce "new programs" designed to actively promote the employees' engagement with the changed company. Between 82 and 88 percent of companies...have not considered or do not choose to implement programs which can yield improved employee performance and confidence.

Warren Boroson
and Linda Burgess,
Across the Board,
11/92

Downsizing is a strategic response to external conditions shaped by internal resources, history, mission, vision and values. It is not a moral choice restricted to the last desperate moment.

3. Making the productivity promise come true

What many executives fail to consider is that downsizing, while a long-term cost savings, requires a short-term investment, beyond incented retirements and separation bonuses. The organization is obliged to invest in the survivors if the productivity promise is to come true.

The investment is both tangible and intangible. On the intangible side there is greater trust of employees at every level. The organization trusts them to:

- accept more responsibility/accountability
- respect the confidentiality of more proprietary information
- make decisions which were formerly made one or two levels above them

At a more tangible level, employees need training on what is required and expected of them in this new environment. They need to be taught how to perform the tasks they now must tackle. They need and deserve recognition and rewards commensurate with their increased value to the organization.

Some of this may be increased compensation for increased performance. Often that is inconsistent with the overall cost-cutting mood of the downsizing organization so employees must settle for recognition and appreciation expressed by their senior leadership. They need more efficient systems and work flows to facilitate higher productivity. They need an organizational culture which fosters cooperation and collaboration rather than internal competition. They need a clear set of priorities to help them make decisions the organization will support when they face tough choices.

The productivity promise is at the core of nearly every downsizing decision. It is an executive responsibility to invest in the employees and systems which will determine if the promise can be met.

4. Rebuilding trust, confidence and commitment

You cannot do more with less. Eventually every executive must realize that you can only do more with more. Yes, you can accomplish more work with fewer people. You can realize greater productivity from a reduced workforce. But those people must have more trust in the organization, more confidence in its leaders and must be more committed to its goals and objectives if they are to do the more that is required.

Again, it falls to the executive level of the organization to build trust, inspire confidence and earn commitment.

Trust has to do with fairness and reliability. We tend to trust those who consistently do what they promise and who treat others from a sense of fair play. Executives must realize that the degree to which they are believed, the degree to which others think them fair-minded, goes a long way in determining their effectiveness.

Confidence comes from the belief that leaders are more than trustworthy. They must also be knowledgeable and intelligent. We must trust their judgment, not just their intentions. Integrity mated to ignorance does not inspire confidence.

Commitment comes from an alignment of the organization's values and those of its employees. The committed employee believes in the value of the organization's contribution to society. They see the organization doing the right things, the right way, for the right reasons.

It is the combination of trust, confidence and commitment that fuels the organization. They are the "mores" that the organization must seek following a downsizing. Doing more with fewer people who have more trust, more confidence and more commitment is a challenging but doable promise.

5. Downsizing redux

Among the many promises that executives make there are inevitably some that there is no hope of keeping. As described above, unkept promises undermine trust. It is tempting for executives to see downsizing as a one-time measure necessitated by unique circumstances. Some are seduced by the power of promising that "This is the last time we expect to have to do this."

That is a meaningless and dangerous promise It recreates the false expectation of lifetime employment all over again. It establishes false hopes and discredits the urgency of rising performance expectations and culture changes.

With the promises of job security and career ladders gone, employees will concentrate on improving their marketability.

The Economist, 4/3/93

The safer promise is one which states that while downsizing is a difficult choice, it may become necessary again. What we, the executives, promise is to do our best to steer this organization intelligently and honorably and avoid downsizing if we can or should. In the process we will invest in our employees to ensure both the organization's optimal success and their future employability either within the organization's bounds or outside.

Executives must face up to the reality of investing in people even when they may not directly recoup all the benefit of that investment. It is an old lesson.

In the 1960s Bell Labs invested heavily in the graduate education of its engineers and scientists. A select few were supported through expensive educational programs leading to doctoral degrees. Each year one or two of these select employees chose to leave Bell Labs. Should Bell Labs continue this level of investment without benefit of some contractual obligation to guarantee a return? The decision was that the value of the program to the organization outweighed the losses associated with those who left. The altruists argued that ultimately they would contribute to society. The pragmatists argued that, more importantly, those who remained were necessary for Bell Labs to fulfill its mission and educating those who left was an acceptable cost of doing business.

Investing in the future employability of employees is rapidly becoming a cost of doing business for those who downsize. For some it is a bargained-for obligation bargained for by unions who realize the importance of lifetime employability, if not lifetime employment. For others it is an enlightened self-interest based on the belief that only through investing in employees can the organization expect them to have the trust, confidence and commitment needed to carry the organization forward to new heights.

Conclusion

In this chapter we looked at a different class of victims of downsizing: the survivors. We identified survivors at three levels: front-line employees and their supervisors/managers, and executives. Finally, we pointed out that each level faces a unique set of issues and discussed what those issues were and why they were important.

In the following chapters we will revisit each of these issues, looking at what the organization might do to address them and how they might do it.

If you have downsized your organization, you now need leadership strategies to make the transition successful.

- *Acknowledge the loss. Your top priority is rebuilding productivity and morale. But where do you start? Begin by acknowledging that employees who remain are just as affected by the downsizing process as those who were laid off.*
- *Propose to make things better. Make a personal decision to see change as an opportunity to make things better.*
- *Get help. Go looking for help. Find employees who share your vision and commitment and make them your "Transition Team."*
- *Listen. Don't assume that the transition team has all the answers (or even all the questions). As their first assignment, have the group "fan out" and gather information from employees as well as internal and external customers.*
- *Focus on vision and values. After the "information gathering" phase, the transition team should draft a transition strategy. Focus first on your vision and values. Vision describes your preferred future and sets the strategic direction in its new form. Values describe the character and quality of the organization and services.*
- *Identify priorities. With vision and values in place, the transition team next turns its focus to priority action planning.*
- *Follow through. People don't resist change. They resist the promise of change followed by "business as usual." This is where most transition plans fall short.*
- *Evaluate and adjust. No plan lasts forever. The environment and circumstances are constantly changing. New opportunities and challenges present themselves.*

Greg Hulsizer, *Executive Excellence, 4/94*

Summary Map

The Other Victims

Other downsizing victims

- front-line employees who keep their jobs
- their supervisors/managers
- executives who remain with the organization

Front-line employees

Issues facing front-line employees who keep their jobs:

- grieving which consists of several stages: denial, anger, blame (others), guilt (self-blame), adaptation/accommodation
- resistance to change because of the disruption of the status quo
- fear of the potential for future disruption and uncertainty
- distrust in an organization that "violates" the social contract of work
- increasing workload which results in the remaining employees doing what they see as more for less
- developing new skills which are necessitated by expansion of the surviving employees' jobs
- decreasing systems support because staff "experts" are frequently the first to go during downsizing
- deciding to recommit in the face of potentially diminished opportunities for leadership and growth

Supervisors/Managers

Issues facing supervisors/managers who keep their jobs:

- They are key employees in the organization's survival effort.
- They face all the issues faced by front-line employees.

Additional issues facing them include:

- diffusing grief and resistance in the employees they oversee
- supporting an unpopular decision
- raising expectations while reducing support
- balancing accountability and authority
- transitioning their employees and themselves into new roles

Executives

Several issues face executives in addition to those already discussed.

The five most prevalent are:

- focusing on the strategy
- facing reality versus preserving myths
- making the productivity promise come true
- rebuilding trust, confidence and commitment
- downsizing redux

Chapter 5

Organizational and Executive Roles and Responsibilities

The phrase "roles and responsibilities" is frequently found in such organizational documents as position descriptions and job evaluations. In most cases the words are used synonomously, as if they were one long word, "rolesandresponsibilities".

Some people attempt to draw a distinction between them. Roles define the parts we play. Much like in a dramatic production, each organizational actor in this drama has an assigned role or set of roles. Our roles define what we do, and when and where we do it. Roles define our place, our relationships with each other and the actions we take.

At the macro level, roles include: executive, manager, supervisor and front-line employee. They are captured by titles such as Chief Financial Officer, Internal Auditor, Customer Service Representative and Computer Programmer.

Responsibilities have more of a flavor of defining the desired outcomes of the role, the results we are trying to achieve. They are aimed more at who and what and when than roles and include more specificity in their definition. Responsibilities are often couched in accomplishment-related terms, or deliverables. So a person may be responsible for maintaining a particular report, building a clearly defined product, writing a specific program or managing a given account.

Yet from a practical point of view, it can be difficult in conversation to differentiate between what is a role and what is a responsibility. So for ease of reading and clarity we will adopt the convention of using "roles and responsibilities" as an all-inclusive catch phrase, just as if the word were, in fact, rolesandresponsibilities.

Personal responsibility

There is a common malady afoot in our culture. It was captured in a recent survey of elementary school teachers in the Los Angeles public school system. These teachers were asked, "What are the most common excuses children offer for not having completed their assigned homework?" The telling response was that the first person singular pronoun "I" did not appear in the top five answers. It was not until you got down to answer number six, "I forgot" that there was any semblance of the student accepting responsibility for their behavior. The five most frequent responses put the blame for not having completed a homework assignment on somebody else. Even "The dog ate it" was reported to be more a commonly used excuse than "I forgot".

The point of the story is this: we need to differentiate between responsibility and blame. We are too accustomed to hearing the question, "Who's responsible for ...?" to mean, "Who can be blamed?" In this context, when we are talking about roles and responsibilities the object is not to assign blame. Rather it is to identify a home, a residence, for a given set of roles and responsibilities so that the incumbent can have greater clarity as to what is expected and/or required for success.

Without role clarity it is impossible to have clearly defined responsibilities. Without clearly defined responsibilities, whether imposed or of our own design, we cannot truly understand what is expected or required, what we are to do or how we are to serve. Our place in the organizational framework is defined by our roles and responsibilities.

It is too common for employees to confront the reality of downsizing by seeking to blame someone or something, to assign responsibility to others for their personal discomfort or inconvenience. Once they get stuck in the blaming mode, progress through the grieving cycle towards adaptation is stymied. "Whose fault is it?" is the wrong question. The more appropriate question after a downsizing is "Who has what responsibilities now?"

Individual responsibility is too important a theme to slight. There are three sets of roles and responsibilities which we discuss in this and the following chapters. They are discussed by level within the organizational hierarchy, but do not be misled. Ultimately, whatever level, whatever role, the responsibility for effective and ethical action is personal. It resides not with the position, but with the person holding the position.

There are also responsibilities which are collective, which naturally accrue to the organization itself, not to any one individual. In these next three chapters we look, therefore, at four sets of roles and responsibilities, those that are of the organization and those that belong to individuals at three hierarchical levels of the organization:

- executives
- supervisors
- individual employees

As we will see, downsizing provides increased opportunities for the assignment and acceptance of responsibility to or by the organization itself, at all levels of the organization.

In these three chapters we will detail several roles and sets of responsibilities for the organization and the three levels of employees for whom issues were defined in the preceding chapters: front-line employees, supervisors and executives. The roles and responsibilities described below are those which seem to be significantly different today, after downsizing, from how the job was defined and done before the downsizing, if the strategy is to be effective.

The combined roles and responsibilities at each level of the organization are such that their effective implementation is a necessary prerequisite to the eventual success of the decision to downsize. Implementing these roles and responsibilities allows, although it cannot guarantee, the realization of the goals and objectives associated with that decision. The failure to accept the responsibility, to enact the roles, or to do so poorly, will almost guarantee that the anticipated goals and objectives will not be realized.

It is the combination of effective implementation of roles and responsibilities at all levels that allows for success. Whatever your level, you are a key player. Together with the other key players you will determine if downsizing will become a strategic success.

Organizational roles and responsibilities

There are some roles and responsibilities which are collective. They belong to the organization. But organizational responsibility can be difficult to define. Though the organization may be an "entity" in legal terms, it is a not a person in the real sense. There is no one individual who *is* the organization so it may be that when we describe some of the organizational responsibilities we are really talking about executive, supervisory or individual responsibilities. But we will continue to use the organization as the locus of these responsibilities since they transcend any level or function. These are really issues of organizational identity and culture and may derive from a variety of sources and levels.

Replacing traditional loyalty with the new glue

The most important organizational responsibility is to create a new glue for holding the organization together. Prior to downsizing the most common basis for employee commitment to the organization has been the concept of loyalty. Sometimes this has been loyalty to an individual leader. Sometimes employees have loyalty to a customer base or to the body of work. But most often the organization has been the focus for employee loyalty. It is the employee's sense of loyalty to the organization that is the binding agent. It is what makes the employee come to work on those days where the decision to get out of bed is in question. Loyalty is the motivator, the little kick in the seat that tells us we should do what we might not necessarily feel like doing.

Loyalty is also one of the early victims of downsizing. Truth and trust may be the first victims, but loyalty, a manifestation of perceived mutual trust, is not far behind.

What is loyalty? It is one consequence of a mutual sense of obligation resulting from the predictable behaviors of both the organization and the employee. It is the natural result of the social contract of work being enforced. Loyalty is what happens when the employee believes that the organization will act in his or her best interest and is therefore motivated to act in the organization's best interest. It is the organizational glue that holds employees. The social contract of work promised that in exchange for the employee's loyalty to the organization, the organization, in return, would be loyal to the employee. The organization would provide continuing, even lifetime, employment. Loyalty was the glue. Lifetime employment was the promise. No more. Downsizing undermines loyalty as thoroughly as any other organizational choice. The glue that was loyalty ceases to hold employees and organizations together.

When that social contract is rescinded unilaterally by the organization, trust is violated and loyalty sacrificed. That raises the question of what the organization can substitute as an alternative glue to bind the employee to the organization once loyalty is lost.

That organizations have traditionally valued and honored employee loyalty is beyond a doubt. Just look at the operating procedures of nearly every large employer in North America. There are written rules for how to celebrate service anniversaries. The five-year pin, the ten-year pin, all the way up to the fifty-year gold watch are symbols of the sanctity of loyalty as an organizational institution. These are the milestones that nearly every organization honors. In fact, most large, mature organizations have authorized budget for the commemoratives associated with service anniversaries. They typically do not authorize the expenditure of organization funds to celebrate promotions or other personal milestones, just service anniversaries. The message to the casual observer is clear, "We value loyalty".

Top executives also need to spell out which of the company's traditional values will be preserved, says Dr. Gerald Kraines. Lifetime loyalty to employees is gone. What else is out the window?

Lee Smith,
Fortune,
7/25/94

When the first downsizing comes, the feeling of betrayal is heightened by the contrast between this new imperative to do everything faster, better and cheaper with fewer people and the tradition of honoring and respecting a person's tenure and loyalty to the organization.

Loyalty was once the basis for employee commitment to organizational goals and objectives. If I am loyal to the organization then I will support its goals and objectives. That, after all, is how I demonstrate my loyalty. Commitment to organizational goals and objectives is second only to staying with the organization as an indicator of loyalty.

What then is the new glue? We see ethical congruence and the promise of lifetime employability as the replacements for loyalty as the new binding elements, the new bases for commitment to an organization that can no longer be expected to honor loyalty with the promise of lifetime employment.

Ethical congruence

Congruence is a concept borrowed from plane geometry. When two figures are congruent they are of the same size and shape. If one were placed on top of the other they would align perfectly with no overlapping, no hangovers.

Ethical congruence is the organizational state where the professed values of the organization (what it says it believes in), the operational values (those that can be inferred from the organization's behavior) and the personal values of the individual employee (how he/she defines right, fair and good) are significantly, if not perfectly, aligned. This is the condition where the employee can agree with and support the values underlying the decisions and actions of the organization. Where he or she can therefore support the decision or action itself.

For example, consider the service representative in the customer service center. This person believes in treating customers fairly. The organization says that it too believes in treating the customer fairly. And it creates systems and structures, measurements and rewards, priorities and decision-making guidelines that make it easier for the service representative to treat the customer fairly. That is ethical congruence.

The employee now finds it easier to commit to the goals and objectives of the organization because these goals and objectives represent commonly held values. Rather than support the choices of the organization out of a sense of loyalty, today's employee will support the organization out of a belief that they operate from a common agenda, shared values and ethical congruence.

Lifetime employability

The old promise inherent in mutual loyalty was lifetime employment. Employment is how the organization expresses loyalty to one of its employees. In exchange for continuing presence and support the organization offers the ongoing opportunity to do the organization's work. By now the reader surely realizes that the promise of lifetime employment cannot be made in good conscience. External forces are too unpredictable and volatile to allow any organization, with the possible exception of the church, to hold that promise out. There may still be employees who go to work for one organization and remain there for their entire work lives. They are the exceptions. Lifetime employment will continue to happen but it can no longer be the overriding assumption of the contemporary social contract of work.

One alternative promise is employability. The organization's obligation to its employees has not gone away. It has merely transmuted and taken a new form. Where once the organization implied a promise of employment, it must make a new promise. And a promise must be made. Employees need a promise if they are to commit to the organization's agenda. Ethical congruence is a necessary but insufficient precondition for commitment. It makes it possible for the employee to commit. The promise must be offered and believed if the employees are to decide to commit.

All too often, companies ignore survivors because they're caught in a catch-22: they've downsized for monetary reasons, and instituting programs for remaining employees costs money they feel they just can't spare.

Warren Boroson and Linda Burgess, *Across the Board*, 11/92

Lifetime employability as a promise is an acceptable alternative to lifetime employment. It promises that "If we cannot keep you, at least you will have a marketable set of skills and competencies when we let you go." Among the risks, of course, is that if employees are eminently marketable, then the market may act and the organization may lose valuable employees at the time of their choosing, rather than the organization's.

That is one organizational cost of breaking the bonds of loyalty. One other is the cost of fulfilling the promise of lifetime employability, which typically means an ongoing investment in training and education for all employees beyond the minimum necessary to ensure adequate performance in the current job. As described in Chapter 4, the paradox is that immediately following a downsizing, the cost per employee goes up. A sizable part of that increase is the necessity to invest in employee training. That investment is a function of both the need for employees to learn new skills and competencies to succeed in the new, more demanding job that downsizing has produced and the cost of maintaining their employability and/or marketability as the promise replacing the lifetime employment promise held forth in the now defunct social contract of work.

Executive roles and responsibilities

As noted in Chapter 4 executives have a strategic responsibility. They are responsible for attending to the mission, vision, values, goals, objectives and strategic plans of the organization. Downsizing is, in those cases where it is the optimal response to the opportunities and constraints present in the organization's environment, resources and history, both the output of and input to a strategy. It is a response to demands on the organization and becomes, itself, a set of demands requiring still further responses.

Notable among all of the executive's responsibilities immediately following the decision to downsize are three:

- separating the baby from the bath water
- creating the norms needed for today's success
- setting the stage for tomorrow's success

The "baby" in this context refers to the essential work of the organization, the essential formal systems, the essential informal systems. This is what we will refer to as the "essential agenda", and it is this essential agenda that senior management needs to be attending to.

The "bath water" is the nonessential agenda. This includes the formal and informal systems that were used to maintain the status quo in the predownsizing environment but which no longer are effective in supporting the new emerging status quo. A simple example should suffice to illustrate the bath water notion: service anniversary commemorative celebrations.

As described earlier, employee loyalty typically was measured in years of service. Milestone service anniversaries were celebrated with gifts, plaques, letters, speeches and all variety of festivities. In a loyalty-focused organizational culture that was essential. In a downsized organization, where loyalty has been supplanted by ethical congruence and where the basis for commitment to goals and objectives is shared values, rather than accrued tenure, elaborately celebrating service anniversaries sends a counterproductive message. It confuses rather than clarifies.

It is an executive level responsibility to develop a plan for migrating the organization away from outdated norms and replacing them with norms which are more timely and appropriate.

Looking at the formal system, it may be necessary to rewrite the policy covering service anniversary celebrations and awards. Rather than do away with all such awards and celebrations it may be wise to phase them out over a period of years. The policy may choose to de-emphasize five- and ten–year anniversaries. A simple acknowledgment from the immediate supervisor accompanied by a commemorative certificate may suffice. New employees are operating from a different set of assumptions and may not care as much. The policy may retain a scaled down budget to celebrate 20 or more years in recognition with a bit more hoopla. The reality is that those employees probably cared deeply about mutual loyalty at some point and would be hurt unnecessarily if all recognition of tenure/loyalty were done away with.

The informal systems also recognized tenure. Seniority was one way of selecting future supervisors or determining who would get their choice of assignments. There was a sense in some organizations that a given individual had earned a promotion by virtue of having the longest tenure in the subordinate job. Supervisors would hold out the promise of promotion based on tenure.

Rarely was there a formal policy that stated loyalty/tenure would be rewarded. It just became practice over the years, a tradition of honoring loyal employees, of rewarding loyalty with a better paying job, the better assignments, the preferred opportunity. Seniority carried with it specific, albeit informal, entitlements. In one construction company, for example, the senior employees always got the new trucks. It was a reward for loyalty.

Senior employees would get preferential treatment in the assignment of work or schedules. This is an informal phenomenon to the extent that it is not dictated by a contract or policy. Of course, in some organizations, the unions have successfully negotiated for a number of otherwise informal decisions being tenure-based. The seniority basis of many union working agreements is a codification of the significance of loyalty under the previous social contract of work.

Executives need to be aware of which operating norms, whether formally or informally based, need to be retained and which need to be discarded. They need to consciously and deliberately define the essential agenda for the downsized organization. They must also recognize that once defined, that essential agenda, like the prior social contract, is subject to change. Today's essential agenda is not going to serve well as tomorrow's. The executive responsibility to be the strategic thinkers for the organization does not stop once an essential agenda has been defined.

Consider the essential agenda associated with the prevalent supervisory style used within the organization. In a traditional organization a somewhat directive supervisory style may have been acceptable. In a downsized organization, with fewer levels, broader spans of control and lower level decision making becoming operational necessities, directing an employee

Michael Walsh, CEO of Tenneco, cut 9,000 jobs world wide—about 10 per cent of the company's payroll.

Managers routinely worked 14-hour days, often six days a week, to eke out the gains.

In Walsh's first year, Tenneco shrank from nine levels of management to three, at the managers' own suggestion.

Walsh believes those in the middle won't willingly break their backs unless the Big Guy is doing the same and everyone knows it—a circumstance he calls "visible and vulnerable" leadership.

Anne B. Fisher,
Fortune,
11/30/92

as to the what, when, where and how of the job might best be reserved for those cases where the employee is unfamiliar with the task at hand. A more participative style of leadership may be a functional necessity in cases where the employee is competent and committed.

Executives are responsible for deciding on more than the agenda itself. They have to define the appropriate formal and informal systems needed to support the desired organizational culture and climate that make up the essential agenda.

The alternative is to abdicate this responsibility. In some organizations executives have allowed the random forces at work within the organization to create the context within which the work is performed based on norms that emerged without the benefit of rhyme or reason, by chance rather than by strategic design.

One tool for assisting executives in this responsibility is the climate survey, sometimes called the employee attitude survey. This tool can be built around a series of statements which collectively define the essential agenda of the organization.

One way to maximize the value of this assessment is to have each respondent describe two aspects for each element of the survey. Using a numerical scale, each respondent can indicate how *important* each element listed in the survey is, and how *effectively* they believe the organization is implementing or managing that element.

This value of maintaining a strategic focus and the continuing development of an up-to-date definition of the organization's essential agenda cannot be overstated. That, after all, is what being an executive is all about. All the organization's stakeholders entrust executive leadership with the responsibility to pilot the organizational ship through the uncharted and turbulent waters of the ever-changing environment and to effectively utilize the organization's resources to achieve its strategic goals and objectives. When executives divert their attention from that task they are derelict in their responsibility and risk having the metaphorical ship crash on the not-so-metaphorical rocks of competition, regulation, worker unrest, and lack of clarity of and commitment to mission, vision and values.

Other executive roles and responsibilities include:

- redefining the culture
- communicating the new vision
- building the new systems
- moving from rules-based to values-based decision making
- letting go of tactical control

Redefining the culture

Downsizing, almost by definition, stimulates a culture change in almost every organization. It represents a deliberate move away from one tradition and constitutes the first steps in establishing a new tradition. The problem is that this is too often an unanticipated aftereffect, not the deliberate, desired or anticipated outcome of the downsizing.

Redefining the culture is an executive responsibility. The steps needed to redefine the culture cannot be carried out at any other level. Others may be involved in the specific implementation of any of these steps, but it is the executive who must assume the role of speaker for the organization and definer of its culture.

Redefining a culture has, as a matter of history, seven components. This is not a prescription for effective culture change. Rather it is a description and explanation of what seems to happen in those cases where culture actually changes. The seven steps are shown here in approximate chronological order. You will notice in reviewing them that their order of importance is roughly opposite to their chronology. It is the last items that are highest priority. While all seven steps appear essential, the last two are the make it or break it steps that are too often overlooked or mismanaged. The seven steps are:

- formal statements of philosophy
- education and training
- formal (organizational) systems
- informal (leadership) systems
- rewards

- reaction to critical events
- senior management focus

1. Formal statements of philosophy

These are the organization's official communications of its position on the issue, such as statements of organizational values, policy statements or announcements of major "cultural" initiatives (e.g. total quality management, ethics, empowerment, customer satisfaction).

In the downsized organization assumptions about priorities, goals and purpose can all become confused. It is up to the executive leadership to clarify these philosophical keystones. It is an inherent part of their role to define and communicate the organization's philosophical positions and to show how the recent downsizing is consistent with the current operational philosophy. Executives need to demonstrate that the stated philosophy and the decision and actions of the organization's leaders are consistent. They must demonstrate that the decision to downsize is representative of the new culture, not merely an aberration or violation of the old culture.

Communicating the philosophy is necessary. The typical pattern for communication in many organizations of "print, post and pray" (print up the formal statement, post it to the plant or office walls and pray for something to happen) does little to bring change about. When only this step is completed, both awareness *and* skepticism/cynicism about the issue increase.

2. Education and training

Education and training are the primary communications vehicles used by many organizations to "get the word out". They allow for information to be shared and associated skills to be developed. But these are not what cause change. Rather they *facilitate* change caused by the remaining five items. Training, when not supported by the remaining items, is a "flea dip" (where one treats a cat or dog for fleas, but does nothing to remove the fleas from the environment, ensuring that the treatment will have no long-term effect). To be optimally effective, training has to start at the top. The hardest question to answer in the classroom is, "Has my boss seen this?" when you know that the boss has no idea of what is being said in the classroom. As training "cascades" down the organization, management support must be active and visible.

3. Formal (organizational) systems

It is systems like organizational structure, job design, methods, procedures, goal and objective setting, data management and quality control that determine what people do day-in and day-out. When systems support change, change happens. When systems are not updated to support desired change, change doesn't happen easily. It is policy and procedure which drive the bureaucratic middle-management levels of organizations. Failure to change these systems means that change will be actively resisted by those people driven by conformance to systems. One of the most obvious systems has to do with temporary or adjunct assignments in support of the desired change. If committees or teams are needed, how are they structured, funded and managed?

4. Informal (leadership) systems

Informal systems (leadership behavior and operational norms) are different from formal organizational systems because of their greater impact on employee behavior. How are people treated? Who gets hired, transferred, promoted or placed in particular openings? What does my immediate supervisor really expect and require? How should I really act? The answers to these questions tell about what the organization truly values. If the informal systems support the formal philosophy, that philosophy is reinforced. If the informal systems contradict or ignore the philosophy then most people feel safe disregarding the stated philosophy. Informal norms and leadership behavior shape employee behavior more than stated philosophy, training or formal systems and structures.

5. Rewards

Of all the organization's systems, rewards (and their implied measurements) are the most powerful. This is how the organization "puts its money where its mouth is". Many people will suspend judgment of the organization's professed intentions until after they see how the organization treats those who accepted the message and acted on it. The skeptics, in particular, judge commitment by how formal and informal rewards are allocated.

6. Reaction to critical events

What does the organization do *vis à vis* its professed commitment when times get tough? Does commitment to the stated philosophy seem to waver in the face of budget cuts, layoffs, increased competition or other dire circumstances? People pay attention to the degree to which the organization demonstrates commitment to fundamental values, especially in times of crisis. This is the acid test of the organization "walking the talk" or "staying the course" when it would be easier to revert to the way things used to be.

7. Senior management focus

Do people believe that management really cares about the stated philosophy? What does senior management care about most? What gets the big boss angry? What makes him/her happy? What is the top priority item on the weekly staff meeting agenda? What never gets talked about? These are the questions that indicate top management's real focus. People want to know that focus because success in what matters counts more than success in what nobody at the top cares about. If the message is ambiguous, people will presume a focus and communicate it through the organization's grapevine.

In asking some employees to leave, open communication is essential from the outset, says management consultant Larry Lee. Workers need to know the truth about their situation. Most people are reasonable when they understand why certain decisions have to be made.

Christopher Ryan, *Ingram's*, 9/93

Communicating the new vision

One of the critical roles for executives is communicator of the new vision. This is not a case of words alone. Executives, perhaps more than any other class of employee, are carefully watched by those who believe that their individual success is inexorably entwined with their ability to divine the wants and needs, wishes and desires of those above them in the organizational hierarchy.

Executives communicate their operating philosophy by every word and deed. Their presumed vision is that which can be inferred and supported by the weight of their actions. It is the executive who leads by example and must "walk the talk" .

Early research on adult communication suggested that words are actually less influential than nonverbal communications, including decisions and actions. More recently, according to Myers and Myers (writing in *The Dynamics of Human Communication*, 1992) the presumption of which communications form is more influential has come under renewed scrutiny. There is widespread agreement, however, that people find incongruence between the spoken word and nonverbal communication to be disruptive at best and indicative of the speaker's lack of trustworthiness at worst. So if executives want to communicate a new vision and have their communication believed, congruence of word and deed is a plus.

Building the new systems

It is unreasonable to expect a new culture to emerge without the development of the required supporting systems. The three levels of systems—formal organizational systems, informal systems and leadership behaviors—and the critical measurements and rewards mentioned above as the core of systemic change are an executive responsibility.

Executives are not expected to create the systems, write the policies or revise the standard operating procedures. Rather, they are expected to provide the impetus for their development, implementation and effective utilization. That is done when the development of the needed systems is part of the critical agenda, when executive-level management makes it clear to the rest of the organization that the development, implementation and use of these systems as the basis for doing business is their concern.

It is the executives who need to set this series of events in motion. If they fail to do so the organization will be stymied by the mixed message inherent in the new stated philosophy being contradicted by a continuing reliance on the previously existing formal and informal systems. When that contradiction is observed the most common interpretation is that the verbiage can safely be ignored, and that despite what anyone might be saying, the rules for doing business remain unchanged. Business as usual becomes the path of least resistance for an organization that naturally obeys the laws of inertia. For the organization to change direction requires the application of executive force, as evidenced by changing organizational systems, sufficient to overcome the resistance inherent in the organization's history, traditions, norms and prior culture.

Moving from rules-based to values-based decision making

Often, when organizations downsize they push the site for decision making to lower hierarchical levels. This changing of the location for decision making is not always understood by the very executives who choose it as a definition of the new status quo. The part that is not clearly seen is that a fundamental shift in the basis for decision making is needed if the shift in the locus of decision making is to be effective.

The nature of that shift is simple to describe. People are being asked to make decisions that they have never had to make before. Their first tendency is to seek guidance from rules or precedence as they endeavor to make decisions that the organization will judge acceptable. That is the safe course—just do what has been successfully done in the past.

If the organization were not in the midst of a downsizing, that might be an effective strategy for some decisions. But in the downsizing organization, there rarely are effective precedents or applicable rules to guide decision makers.

In fact, reliance on rules or precedents is often directly opposite to what is needed to meet the changing demands on the organization and the decision maker.

The preferred alternative is reliance on goals, consistent with principles or values. If the decision maker has a clear understanding of what the organization is trying to accomplish and has a clear sense of what the organization believes in and values, then he or she can make an effective decision or choice between competing alternatives with a high degree of confidence that the decision will be supported by the organization.

It becomes an executive responsibility to do two things to support this shift in the basis for decision making.

Executives must clearly communicate the principles and values they want employees to rely upon when faced with decisions for which there is not a relevant precedent or policy.

They must also guarantee the safety of the decision maker. They must promise that if the decision maker effectively applies the stated principles and values to the available data, the decision maker will be supported, even if, after the fact, the decision itself cannot be.

Letting go of tactical control

The last executive responsibility we will discuss is the need for executives to remain strategically focused and to relinquish their tight rein on the day-to-day tactical decisions that their direct reporting employees must make in the downsized organization.

One of the promises of downsizing is an organization that is more efficient and can respond faster to change. That requires executive attention be focused on the forces of change and the development of the organizational capacity to adapt.

It is not reasonable to expect this level of organizational agility if senior and midlevel managers are not given the freedom to accomplish the strategic goals of the organization, consistent with the stated principles and values, without having to run every tactical decision past the "top dogs" for review, input and approval. The notion that executives have to "put their mark" on every tactical decision is archaic, yet some organizations are still hindered by executives who believe their role is to "mark their territory" by putting their distinctive scent on every tactical decision.

These executives must realize that they have a larger role to play. They are there to lead. Their role is to ensure that the message of mission, vision and values is clear and understood and that it is appropriate for the challenges and opportunities present in the organization's operating environment. The doing of the organization's work is the role and responsibility of their employees.

Those roles, in the newly downsized organization, are detailed in the following chapters.

I recommend that executives learn to drive strategy and lead people through 10 checkpoints of strategic leadership:

Step 1. Understand the environment.

Step 2. Revisit the mission.

Step 3. Answer three fundamental Drucker questions: What is our business? Who is our customer? and What does the customer consider value?

Step 4. Communicate the vision.

Step 5. Ban the hierarchy.

Step 6. Challenge the gospel.

Step 7. Dispersed leadership.

Step 8. No matter what you call it—just do it.

Step 9. The power of language.

Step 10. Lead from the front.

The first responsibility of a leader is to define reality. The last is to say "thank you." In between, the leader is a servant.

Frances Hesselbein, *Executive Excellence*, 8/94

Summary Map

Executive Roles and Responsibilities

Role

The part each employee plays

Responsibility

What is expected or required

Personal responsibility

Employees and others often confuse personal responsibility with blame. Personal responsibility is the willingness to accept ownership of a role and the charge for completion of the tasks and duties associated with filling that role.

Organizational roles and responsibilities

Those roles and responsibilities which are collective and belong to the organization

Levels of organizational responsibility

Organizational responsibilities may fall at any level:

- executive
- manager/supervisor
- front-line employee

While identified as collective responsibilities (the organization may be an entity in the "legal" sense although it is not a person), organizational responsibilities are also someone's personal responsibilities.

Traditional versus new loyalty

The most important organizational responsibility associated with downsizing is to create new "glue" to hold the organization together. Loyalty provides the motivation to keep moving when faced with obstacles.

Ethical congruence

The organizational state where the professed values of the organization (what it says it believes in), the operational values (those inferred from the organization's behavior), and the personal values of employees (how the employee defines right, fair and good) are aligned.

Lifetime employability

Once a "promise" as part of the social contract of work, employees perceive continued employment as a sign of the organization's loyalty. Changing work situations make the guarantee of lifetime employment a thing of the past.

Executive strategic responsibilities

An organization's executives are always responsible for:

- mission
- vision
- values
- goals
- objectives
- strategic plans

Executive downsizing responsibilities

Immediately following the decision to downsize, executives pick up three additional responsibilities:

- separating the essential work of the organization from nonessential work
- migrating the organization away from outdated norms and replacing them with more timely norms
- setting the stage for future success by maintaining a strategic focus

Other executive responsibilities

- Redefine the culture by:

— Establishing formal statements of organizational philosophy

— Providing education and training

— Establishing a workable formal system for getting jobs done

— Providing informal systems through leadership, behavior and operational norms

— Installing a rewards systems (this implies measurements also)

— Maintaining commitment to fundamental values when the going gets tough

— Keeping senior management focused on the organization's stated philosophy

- Communicate the new vision.
- Build new systems.
- Move from rules-based to value-based decision making (a requirement when decision making is pushed down to lower hierarchical levels).
- Let go of tactical control.

Chapter 6

Manager/Supervisor Roles and Responsibilities

The organizational act of downsizing puts supervisors in a unique position. They are employees and share the roles and responsibilities of downsized employees. They are leaders and share some of the downsizing implementation responsibilities for what are typically seen as executive roles and responsibilities. Plus, as supervisors, they have roles and responsibilities unique to that position in the newly reshaped organizational structure. It is these uniquely supervisory roles that are the subject of this chapter.

Supervisory roles and responsibilities

Perhaps the most significant role and responsibility that supervisors face in the downsized organization is that of helping their employees change mindsets. They can ease the transition from employee commitment based on a belief in mutual loyalty to commitment based on employee belief that the organization's goals and objectives are worth supporting. Managers and supervisors need to help their employees move from dependency and a sense of entitlement based on the now mythical social contract of work to the promise of lifetime employability and congruence of beliefs and values as the basis for commitment to the organization and its goals.

These managers and supervisors also need an understanding of employee motivation. They must be tuned into how the rewards inherent in the work of the downsized organization, as well as those rewards provided by the formal and informal systems, can meet the changing needs and expectations of their employees.

They have an additional responsibility of facilitating their employees' development of those skills and competencies necessary for both today's job demands and those needed to realize the new promise of lifetime employability. They must be the coaches and counselors that employees need as they seek to develop competency and employability.

Supervisors must take a stand and decide if they, themselves, choose to be transparent or substantive members of the management team. They need to consider what posture they wish to take regarding the mission, vision, values, goals and objectives of their employer. They must decide what it means to be a member of the management team and to what extent they accept those specific roles and responsibilities.

Finally, they need to become the most dependable source of honest and accurate information available to their employees. They need to be reliable sources of information that employees are willing to trust if they are to be effective in the downsized organization.

From loyalty to commitment

The supervisors' responsibility in the transition of their employees from loyalty-based affiliations to commitment-based affiliations is fairly straightforward. If they do not facilitate the transition it will most likely not occur or will occur very slowly, with any number of detours, delays and missteps. Supervisors are the most visible and influential management representative to the average employee. They are a focal point during the transition period following downsizing. It is supervisors who model the new basis for affiliation with the organization through their actions and decisions.

While the responsibility might be clear, the facilitation task itself is subtle and complex. It requires that the supervisor be able to adequately explain, demonstrate and model the differences between:

commitment based on a perception of mutual loyalty and a social contract of work	versus	commitment based on congruent values, acceptable goals and objectives and the promise of future employability

These are manageable concepts on paper or in the classroom, but they can get fuzzy in real life. Ideally, supervisors should have access to four things if they are to facilitate their own movement through this transition and that of their employees:

1. a process for articulating the organizational and personal values inherent in any given action or decision
2. a process for clearly identifying the goals or objectives for any given action or decision
3. a process for articulating the skills and knowledge required to achieve those goals and objectives
4. a reasonable understanding of the transferability or desirability of those skills and that knowledge in the general employment market

That is a lot to ask of a supervisor. It is not reasonable to expect that every supervisor will be able to address all of those needs each and every time a decision or action is called for. Fortunately, that depth of understanding, while ideal, is not necessary.

The processes for articulating values and goals are simple and readily accessible. They can be found in any of a dozen ethical decision-making models. One simple model was suggested by Sanford Krolick several years ago in his work on ethical decision making. Krolick proposed that any decision or action had four components. Decision makers look at all four sets of considerations but may afford them differing degrees of significance depending on the decision maker and the situation. The four considerations are:

1. Individualism—what would be the impact of the action or decision on the actor or decision maker?
2. Altruism— what would be the impact of the action or decision on others and on the relationship between those others and the actor or decision maker?

3. Pragmatism—what would be the practical impact of the action or decision on the business?

4. Idealism— is the action or decision right, fair and good?

This type of analysis affords the supervisor a vehicle for identifying the values, goals and objectives in a given decision or action using a simple four-word formula: Individualistic, Altruistic, Pragmatic, Idealistic.

As for the skills and knowledge requirements, that should not pose any problems. Supervisors traditionally needed to be able to identify the skills and knowledge requirements of any task as well as those possessed by the employee if they were to reasonably assign work and define the degree of autonomy or freedom the employee would be allowed in the performance of the work.

They also had the traditional role of identifying areas for improvement. They were the ones employees looked to for guidance in what was required for continuing effectiveness and success on the job.

Perhaps the greatest challenge is in appreciating the marketability of a set of skills and knowledge. That requires an understanding of what is going on outside the organizational boundaries, an appreciation of the industry and other related fields. Thus we have defined one of the skills and knowledge areas that supervisors need to develop to be effective in today's redefined organization that might not have been necessary before.

Middle management who report:

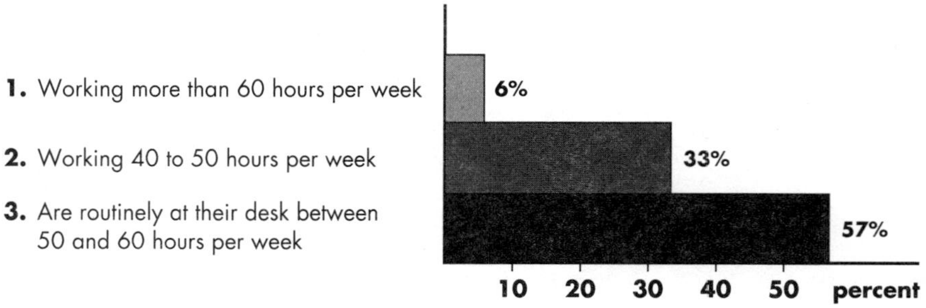

From a poll of 1,344 middle managers reported in *Fortune* 11/30/92.

This knowledge is attainable but requires that the supervisor broaden his or her horizons. Some simple tactics can be useful:

- subscribe to and read industry journals
- read the want ads
- read your own organization's advertisements for employees at various levels
- read the placement ads, both job offers and positions wanted, in industry, trade or professional association newsletters

This is a challenging responsibility for two reasons. It is daunting in that it requires a redefinition of the supervisor's role. It is imposing in that it requires the supervisor to accumulate new insights and wisdom often without the benefit of any formal support from the organization.

These demands are further complicated by the fact that they present themselves when the supervisor is probably busier and more stretched in his or her supervisory experience than ever before. This means that the average supervisor is likely to relegate this particular responsibility, defining future employability, to the back burner. It is likely to be viewed as necessary but not urgent.

It appears to be the exception that supervisors are taking this responsibility seriously. The onus for changing that falls on their supervisors, those more senior managers who define the priorities and success criteria that front-line supervisors use to guide themselves in priority setting and decision making.

But the absence of top-down pressure to deal with employee employability is no excuse. This responsibility sits squarely on the shoulders of every supervisor. One can argue that the ultimate responsibility should rest with the employee. After all, it is the employee's future that is at stake, not the supervisor's.

While that is true, there is a fairness factor that we are taking into consideration. The organization has a responsibility to substitute employability for the withdrawn promise of employment. The supervisor is the organization's agent in this regard. While the employee is the beneficiary, the organization, and thus the supervisor, cannot sit idly by watching while the employee struggles to define what the future will require. Supervisors have access to that world view and thus the responsibility to share, guide, direct and lead.

Motivating employees

Not surprisingly, perpetual downsizing can take a heavy toll on employee morale. "Better to bite the bullet and get the whole downsizing out of the way," says Harry Levinson, who heads the Levinson Institute in Bellmont, Massachusetts, "then you can assure the survivors it's really over."

Warren Boroson and Linda Burgess, *Across the Board,* 11/92

Motivation is a subject that has fascinated supervisors since the Romans first divided their legions into groups of ten. In the past it was a simple process. Fear was the motivator. Do what you are told or die. That was simple enough for everyone to understand. No codes of conduct need be written. No employee handbooks. No policy manuals. Just do it, or else.

Early into the industrial age the same process carried forward. However, starting in the 1920s motivation became a topic of more diverse interest as punishing one employee to make an example and to keep others in line was decreasingly socially acceptable. Employees came to believe that they had rights. Employers came to believe that they had to motivate their employees.

Fear remained a primary motivational tool. Do what you are told or you will be fired. That actually held up through the Great Depression. But somewhere in the middle of this century, as employee rights became firmly entrenched in the social conscience, fear began to fall out of favor as the motivator of choice.

The enlightened management theories of the 1950s and 1960s suggested that employees were better motivated by other things such as the opportunity for success, recognition of work well done, and the chance to perform increasingly meaningful work.

But whether it was fear or enlightenment, the supervisor was seen as the person, other than the employee himself or herself, most responsible for maintaining motivation and morale in the workplace.

One quick aside. Motivation is used here to describe the degree to which the employee wants to do the job at hand. Morale refers to how the employee feels about the organization and the work. They are not the same thing, nor are they inextricably tied to each other. It is possible to have low morale in a highly motivated group and vice versa.

In the downsized organization fear re-emerges, as the view of the future at work becomes increasingly uncertain and frightening. There is a terrible temptation facing the unscrupulous organization or supervisor to revert to fear-based management. One problem with that choice is that employees now have the means to fight back. There is a legal system which affords protections from "wrongful dismissal" among other things. There is also a social sense of fairness, an ethic, that says employees should not be arbitrarily threatened as a means of motivating them to perform routine work. So reverting to fear-based motivation is one temptation that should be resisted.

The assumption for decades has been that loyalty would suffice as a motivator in lieu of fear. Now with loyalty supplanted by downsizing, how is the supervisor to motivate his or her employees? The best understanding we have today is called expectancy theory. The theory suggests that an employee will be motivated to perform a given task if four preconditions exist:

1. Employees must know what is required to perform the task. They must know what particular skills, knowledge and abilities are needed for the successful completion of the task at hand.

2. Employees must be confident that they have a reasonable likelihood for success if they undertake to perform the task. We tend not to be motivated to perform a task where our chances of success are below whatever personal risk threshold we maintain. In this regard Herzberg was right. Accomplishment is a motivator.

3. Employees must understand the probable consequences or outcomes of successfully completing the task and of not completing the task, or failing in the attempt. They must know with a reasonably high degree of reliability what will result from their efforts. That knowledge extends to what will happen to them, to others and even to the organization itself.

4. Employees must desire those consequences or outcomes. They must be able to look at probable outcomes and the likelihood of success and decide that they value the outcome that will result from their efforts.

When addressing the issue of motivation, the responsibility of the supervisor in the downsized organization is to ensure that the task is clearly defined along all four of these dimensions. Perhaps most important, because of how different it is post-downsizing, the supervisor must be clear on the consequences.

Many of the old promises are no longer operational. Pay raises, promotions, advancement, increased responsibility, even continuing employment are no longer givens for successful performance. The new promise is consistency with shared values, attainment of shared goals and objectives and the continuing development of the basis for future employability.

Again, supervisors can "sweeten the pot" by adding their acknowledgment to the set of rewards. The supervisor's recognition of a job well done can be a powerful motivator. One caution when using praise or recognition as a motivator. They only work when two preconditions are met:

1. The praise or recognition must be deserved. The accomplishment of the task, the delivery of the desired outcome, must be significant enough to warrant recognition.
2. The recognition must be sincerely offered. The accomplishment must be of sufficient value to the supervisor that the praise or recognition can be offered with integrity.

Shallow, undeserved or mechanical praise is more demotivating than if the supervisor had said or done nothing in response to the employee's accomplishments.

One caution for supervisors. As you fulfill your responsibility for motivating employees check your point of reference. Expectancy theory says the employees' desire to produce the likely consequences is the driver. It is risky to assume that your desires, your motivators and those of your employees are congruent. Stuart Atkins suggested that rather than relying on the traditional Golden Rule, "Do unto others as you would have them do unto you" that we consider this rewrite, "Do unto others as they would have you do unto them."

Peter Herriot, the director of research at Sundridge Park Management Centre near London, predicts, in the future, big firms will have to offer the best professional workers regular opportunities to add to their marketable credentials in order to recruit or retain them, even though this will also increase their ability to jump to another firm.

The Economist, 4/3/93

Remember, as you seek to make it easier for your employees to become motivated to perform the task at hand, it is *their* wants and needs that task performance must satisfy if they are to be motivated. And it is more than just probable, it is unavoidable that they will be motivated by different consequences and outcomes than you.

Facilitating skills development

Here is a dilemma. You, as the immediate supervisor, are responsible for the ongoing development of your direct reporting employees. To complicate matters, after downsizing, you most likely have more subordinate employees than ever before, they are less prepared for the work at hand than before and you have fewer dollars and hours to devote to their training and development than you had in the past.

That does not relieve you of the development responsibility. It merely makes it one more challenge in what has rapidly become a more challenging position than you had ever dreamed possible. The good news is that employee development is becoming one of the few remaining justifications for having supervisors in the organizational structure.

A few helpful hints regarding employee development:

- If you cannot identify a tangible outcome which serves to better prepare the employee for today's task, tomorrow's task or tomorrow's job market, don't invest in the developmental activity.
- Skip any developmental activity that merely promises to provide your employees with answers. Focus on those that provide processes for developing answers. It is the choice between your employees being fed for a day or learning how to feed themselves. Wherever possible, invest in long-term self-sufficiency.
- Avoid any developmental effort that cannot define what successful completion of the program will produce. If you cannot measure the value of the outcome there probably isn't any.
- Remember to look for the developmental or learning potential in every action and decision, especially those that produced unanticipated or undesired outcomes, what we call failures. We learn and remember better from examining our mistakes than from recalling our successes.
- Give employees the opportunity to teach and learn from each other. Your responsibility is to make sure that they develop. You don't have to do all the work yourself. For example, cross-training is a wonderful opportunity to help both the teacher and the learner develop new, marketable skills and competencies. It is also a wonderful confidence booster for the teacher. And it feels good.

Taking a management posture

With all the change and consternation in the downsized organization, each supervisor has to choose a side. Are you going to be a member of the management team or a victim? Which position you take will significantly influence your ability to be effective in accepting and implementing all of the responsibilities described in this chapter.

Consider this example from several years ago. Howard had eleven subordinate managers each of whom had ten or more subordinate supervisors and dozens of front-line employees reporting to them. It was Howard who taught me about transparent managers, managers who had no substance. These were people who acted as conduits for decisions. They chose to be observers rather than assume their place as players in the unfolding drama. And their motives were often petty. They lacked the courage and integrity to take a necessary, but unpopular position. They were more concerned that they be liked or approved of by their employees than effective.

Howard's management team would collectively decide on a necessary but unpopular decision. Some of the managers would then go to the supervisors and employees and say, "Howard is making us do..." They took no responsibility for the decision that they helped to make. They ducked their responsibility and hid behind a lie.

If you are a supervisor or manager, typically you are a member of the management team that has to make any number of tough calls. Some of these decisions are made by others, higher up than you. What are you going to do when it comes time to implement those decisions? Denying your membership on the teams that made the decision hurts you three ways:

First, it weakens your ability to influence future management decisions by presenting you as a weak team member, one who is unwilling to support the necessary, albeit difficult, decisions.

Second, it creates a perception in your employees that you have no influence, no power. It presents you as someone who cannot, rather than one who can. It makes any support you promise sound hollow. It disempowers you in others' eyes.

Third, and perhaps most disconcerting, denying your membership on the management team creates a self-image of someone who cannot influence or control what in fact is within your grasp. It creates a false sense of what you can and cannot do and invariably makes you less effective, undermining your success and weakening you even further.

One manifestation of transparency is the employees' perception that organizational power resides two levels above them. The immediate supervisor is usually viewed as well intentioned but powerless. That perception derives as much from the excuses supervisors offer employees for their own failures as from any reality regarding who has what organizational power. Supervisors tell employees, "I would like to, but they won't let me."

This positioning of the supervisor as the unsuccessful messenger to those who truly possess organizational power is not merely a front-line phenomenon. We have heard corporate vice-presidents, generals and admirals, even CEO's bemoan their lack of personal power and their desire, but inability, to give their employees what they agree those employees deserve.

Those are the complaints and positions of leaders who lack any real understanding of what it means to be powerful, what it means to lead and how one must position oneself regarding management responsibility versus transparency, for long-term effectiveness.

Accepting your rightful place on the management side of the organization is in and of itself an empowering decision. It positions you as a person who can be relied on, both by your employees and by your own management. You are viewed as a person of integrity and courage, willing to accept responsibility for decisions that may be distasteful, but are made in good faith and for good cause. It makes your promises of employee support and advocacy more substantive.

Choosing to act as a member of the management team is empowering. It gives you substance. Rather than transparency, it affords you depth and breadth. You cast a shadow. Your presence is real and must be taken into consideration.

Rebuilding truth and trust

All the above responsibilities derive from a basic assumption: the supervisor is a trusted and respected leader in the downsized organization. That, unfortunately, cannot be blindly presumed to be the case. In many downsized organizations supervisors have not earned the trust or respect of their employees. For some it is a function of being newly reassigned due to restructuring. Others are not trusted because they are seen as upper management's lackeys. For others, their personal management style is seen as authoritarian, self-serving or lacking in integrity.

The resolution of this issue is another example of easy to say and difficult to accomplish. It requires the supervisor to take an active role in rebuilding the employees' trust in the organization, its management and most importantly, in the supervisor him- or herself. Three types of activities seem to be effective in rebuilding trust:

1. Tell the truth

Scrupulously and unflinchingly tell employees the truth. There are no exceptions, no justifications and no rationalizations which suffice to deviate from the position that employees are always entitled to the truth. The fundamental basis of trust in an organization is truth telling. You are your employees' best source for honest, accurate and timely information. The truth is the first essential building block, the foundation, of a trust-based working relationship.

2. Keep your promises

Never make a promise you cannot keep. Never break a promise you have made. It is better to underpromise and overdeliver than to make promises that cannot be kept.

Trust is the residue of promises fulfilled. One broken promise doesn't move you back to square one. It puts you in the hole. That means you must be very careful what you promise. You must be equally careful what you appear to promise. This is not a time for loophole management, for wiggling out of implied promises by sticking to the letter of what was said rather than the spirit of what was perceived. It is sufficient that an employee believed there to have been a promise broken for the trust to be violated.

3. Back your employees

Your position as supervisor is one which allows you to be your employees' advocate to the organization. You can be the one to represent them and their interests to upper management. You can defend them from unwarranted criticism. You can lobby for the resources critical to their success. You can be their agent and protector.

Being perceived as their greatest supporter becomes a basis for trust when two preconditions are satisfied. First it must be deserved support. Their causes must be just, their needs legitimate, their grievances real. Second it must be sincere. Your support must spring from a genuine desire to do what is right, fair and good. It cannot be seen as a facade or a sham. It cannot be an attempt to manipulate their perceptions and create an undeserved trust.

You won't always win. You will not get them everything they want. You will not protect them from every inequity or injustice. It is sufficient that they believe that you are making a good faith effort and that your intentions are honorable.

It is also quite acceptable for you to honestly disagree with your employees—to choose not to support a particular cause or to tilt against a particular windmill. But do so honestly, with integrity and full candor.

A reputation as a truth teller, promise keeper and employee backer will earn you the right to lead and will make it possible for you to effectively fulfill your responsibilities to your employees: to help them through the transition to the new congruence-based loyalty, to keep them motivated to do the organization's work and to help them develop the skills and competencies which will ensure their lifelong employability.

Managing the expanded workload

Finally, we need to mention the supervisor's role and responsibility associated with managing the expanding workload in the downsized organization. As mentioned above, workload expands two ways. There is more of the same work being done by fewer people and there is new and different work to do.

Some of the work that has been done in the area of supervision and leadership suggests an appropriate response. Ken Blanchard's work, in particular his work on situational leadership, offers advice on how to better manage an expanding workload.

Being able to identify who is best suited for a given task is a necessary supervisory skill. The reality of any work group is that employees are not interchangeable organizational parts, despite what might be suggested by common job titles and position descriptions.

The turmoil associated with layoffs harms the survivors of the enterprise as well as the people who lose their jobs. Unless specific tasks are eliminated first, cutting personnel will leave the unit facing the same work load with a smaller staff, an unappealing prospect for any manager.

Paul Firstenberg,
Management Review,
11/93

Each employee is a unique collection of competencies and is motivated by a unique set of wants and needs. Every employee possesses a set of skills, knowledge and competencies that sets them apart from other employees. Each is an individual with a very personal set of strengths and weaknesses.

Similarly, each task has a unique combination of urgency and significance. Each contributes to the overall goals and objectives of the person performing it, the work group and the overall organization in ways which are different from every other task.

Finally, the supervisor's willingness to let go of control and personal relationship with each employee is a variable that deserves consideration. There are often indescribable differences in the levels of confidence and trust—the degree to which the supervisor and employee are comfortable with each other or desire to please each other—that contribute to motivation and commitment.

All of these variables go into the equation for determining how the supervisor will use the human resources available to meet the demands of the expanding workload. The key is to remember that, as a supervisor, you have a wide range of options. There is no one leadership option that is ideal for all situations. Neither are you limited to a choice among four or five widely discussed leadership styles.

The key is flexibility and that means using all the subtle gradients between and among the traditional leadership modes. Empowering employees is the common name given to the process of increasing the levels of support and authority you provide while decreasing the amount of direction and instruction inherent in the assignment of work. Empowerment is not an all or nothing proposition. It is a matter of degree.

Many supervisors resist empowering their employees because they fear a loss of control. If your model is the on-off switch it is no wonder that you fear losing control. Consider the dimmer switch as an alternative model. A dimmer switch suggests the possibility for slight adjustments, turning the "power" up or down as circumstances require, and mostly, it places control squarely in the hand of the person who holds the switch, the supervisor.

It is the supervisor's responsibility to effectively utilize the available leadership options, ranging from the most highly directive management styles to the most democratic, to best invest the resources represented by the employee body. That investment should be optimized to deliver the outcomes that best serve the organization, best meet its goals and objectives and best meet the commitments and promises of the organization to its employees regarding ethical congruence and future employability.

The empowering supervisor

There appear to be 10 components or characteristics that are associated with the empowering supervisor or manager. As we describe each, consider to what extent you agree that this characteristic is desirable, to what extent you regularly demonstrate it and to what extent your employees would agree with your self-assessment.

1. Alternative vision

Empowering leaders have a different vision. They see the world differently from the traditional leader.

In the science fiction of the late 1940s and early 1950s there was a popular vision of the workplace of the future. The entire building was filled with machines because the work of the future was all going to be done by machines. The only two living creatures in this facility were a human being and a dog. The human's job was to take care of the dog, make sure the dog got water and food and exercise. The dog's job was to make sure the human didn't touch any of the machines.

This was an image of the future that said, "We won't have to work, we are going to be released from work." That reality hasn't come to pass and doesn't look like it will any time soon.

Another inappropriate vision is the view that the role of the supervisor or the manager is to stand alone, to be the one who is in charge, to be the one who knows everything.

Sometimes our visions are accurate, sometimes our visions are inaccurate.

The alternative vision shared by empowering leaders points out that no one individual can possibly know everything about any job and, therefore, we are increasingly dependent upon each other. The supervisor cannot know everything about the job and is, therefore, dependent upon the employees.

The employee cannot know everything about the job, so they're more dependent upon each other and upon the supervisor. There is more interdependency now than there used to be.

This vision requires that we work more collaboratively with each other and that we share information, resources and power, because we are dependent on each other for success. I cannot expect you to help me be successful in the long term, unless I'm willing to help you. The vision of the empowering leader is filled with collaboration, cooperation and interdependence.

Empowering leaders also see their role differently. They are not central authority figures, the ones who know it all. Rather, they are the ones who can help get the job done by bringing together all of these other people who know little bits and pieces to collectively create this word that we've heard about since the 1960s, "synergy".

2. Clarity

The key to innovation, creativity and entrepreneurial energy is to turn negative into positive synergy by valuing differences in people.

Steven Covey, *Executive Excellence,* 11/94

Empowering leaders know their strengths and weaknesses. They know what they can do and what they cannot do. As paradoxical as it may sound, they know what their blind spots are and what's in those blind spots. A lot of that has to do with knowing your own styles and proclivities, the things that you want to do because that's what's most comfortable for you. It also means knowing your level of discomfort with uncertainty and how much discomfort you can take.

Empowering leaders tend to associate with people who are very different from themselves. Big picture thinkers surround themselves with people who pay attention to the details. Cautious people seek out risk takers. Quick deciders find deliberaters. And so it goes.

Empowering leaders know their strengths and they know how to fill their gaps with people who are different from themselves, as opposed to cloning themselves. One of the traditional leadership behaviors has been to try to find people who are just like ourselves and populate our organization with little mirror images and little baby clones. The empowering leader is different in that regard.

3. Risk tolerance

Risk tolerance is an interesting process or proposition. Perhaps the best example I ever heard of risk tolerance came out of IBM. It was told by Buck Rogers, author of *The IBM Way*.

Rogers told a story about a young marketing manager. He had made a mistake. It was a sizable mistake that cost IBM two million dollars. His boss chewed him out, told him to never do it again. This was back in the early 1960s; two million dollars in the early sixties was a lot of money. A few days later this young manager was told, "You are to report to the president's office at seven o'clock tomorrow morning."

At seven o'clock the next morning, thinking for sure he's about to be fired for his two-million dollar mistake, he showed up at the president's office. The president said to him, "Young man, I've had my eye on you. You have some things that we're looking for. We have an opportunity to make IBM the number one international marketer of computers. We need someone to put together an international marketing strategy and an international marketing team, to set up our international marketing network and systems, and to go out there and to beat the competition to the world-wide market for computers. And I want you to head up that team."

This represented a huge promotion, raise and tremendous responsibility for the young manager. Besides, this was not what he had expected. He looked at the president and said, "Sir, you know, I really do appreciate it and I'm grateful for the opportunity, but I have tell you, coming in here this morning, I thought you brought me in here to fire me."

And the president of IBM is reported to have said what may be one of the most brilliant things ever said by a CEO anywhere. He looked at him and said, "Fire you? Why on earth would I fire you after I just spent two million dollars training you?"

Empowering leaders recognize that as soon as you start empowering employees, you raise the level of risk. People will make mistakes, people are imperfect. We will fail. I promise.

The question is, how do you respond to that failure. Do you respond to it in such a way that people are encouraged to learn from it and apply their learning, or do you shut them down?

4. High standards

Empowering managers have high standards for themselves and for others, but they stop short of perfectionism. Perfectionism is counter-productive, because that means you always fail. If you pursue excellence instead of perfection, that means you can always succeed and then say, "And the next time we'll do even better."

Tom Peters was absolutely right to title his book *In Search of Excellence*. If he had written *In Search of Perfection*, he would not have had a best seller on his hands.

5. Generous with credit

Every organization claims that its people are its most important resource. And yet, when I ask people how they like the way their performance is evaluated and how they like the way the review system is run, everybody laughs. No one has anything good to say about the appraisal system. This strikes me as strange since there is nothing more vital than making sure that the performance of people is well managed and evaluated.

Ken Blanchard,
Executive Excellence,
10/94

Empowering leaders are the kinds of people who will turn around and say about their employees, "These are the folks who deserve the credit." They sound like a typical awards night in Hollywood: ". . . and I want to thank the little people." But it's true.

Several years ago an upper-level manager won a national sales competition. The 64 people in his organization made his organization number one. He went to the national sales conference, accepted his huge trophy, and stood there and told his peers what *he* had done to deserve their recognition. He never once thanked the 64 people who made him a success. The word got back to his home office in Hialeah, Florida, long before he did. They crucified him. His results went from being number one to number fourteen in a year. They took him down because he hogged the credit.

During an audit in one organization we found one division where the division manager obviously didn't understand the performance evaluation plan. All his outstanding workers, his real stars, were getting "average" evaluations and all his really average people were getting "outstanding" evaluations. We confronted him, asking, "Is there a problem with the plan?"

His explanation was the exact opposite of what an empowering leader would have said. He said, "You never want to give your best people outstanding ratings, because other people see those ratings and take them away from you. They'll promote them out of your organization. You always want to take your best people and give them average ratings so you get to keep them. Give trouble makers the A-plusses so they can go somewhere else and you can get rid of them. They become someone else's problem."

Compare these two stories with a personal hero, Ed Jelks. Ed's position required him to present his "state of the organization" message to the executive council, once a quarter. His favorite thing to do was bring along one of his subordinate managers to present all the good news. He showcased these people and gave them the opportunity to receive credit for the work. Ed was an empowering leader.

6. Lead by example

We have heard "lead by example" all of our lives. "Do as I say, not as I do" doesn't work. You have to live it—you have to "walk the talk".

The true meaning of leading by example really came home about four and a half years ago. Our son, Ian, turned 15. This is a kid who couldn't wait to drive. In Atlanta, Georgia, the age at which you can get a learner's permit, is 15. On his fifteenth birthday, Ian was at the Department of Motor Vehicles getting his learner's permit. That afternoon he was in the car having his first driver's lesson. Dad was the teacher. We were driving through the local neighborhood and came to the end of the street, to a stop sign. He rolled right through the stop sign and made a right hand turn. Dad asked him to pull over and asked if he knew why.

Ian said, "I came to the intersection, I slowed down, I checked the traffic, I made my right turn. I had my right turn signal on. What did I do wrong?"

"Did you notice that big red octagonal sign? The one that said STOP right across the middle?" He said, "Of course."

"What does STOP mean? It does not mean slow down, check for traffic. No, that's what YIELD means. That says STOP. It is not a suggestion. It is the law. You have to come to a full stop."

He looked across the driver's seat and said, "Dad, how long have you been driving?"

"I don't know, 30-something years."

He said, "You know, I can't vouch for all of them, but I can vouch for 15 of them. You never stop at that sign. You never stop unless there's traffic coming."

We lead by example, even when we don't think we're leading by example, because our employees keep watching us.

7. Believe in people

The empowering leader genuinely believes that, given the opportunity, most people will do the best they can, and that the best they can do is pretty darn good. They all need some support, encouragement, help, information and tools. But given the choice, most people will do the right thing.

8. Value diversity

Empowering leaders value diversity, not only in people, but in ideas. They believe that in business there's usually more than one right answer to any problem, and that it is okay for someone to have a different right answer than you have. And so if Shirley is working for me and I ask her to perform a task and she does it differently than I would have, and the outcome is still good, then the fact that she took a different path to get there is a plus, not a minus. We can all learn something from the new approach to solving an old problem. We now know there's another option. So diversity is much broader than nationality, age, race or gender.

9. Encourage sharing

Sharing is critical to the empowering leader, especially the sharing of information, ideas and solutions. We all benefit from sharing the little tricks of the trade, the things that we learn through experience. Empowering leaders encourage each other and they encourage their employees.

One of their strengths is that they encourage everyone to teach each other what we've learned and share what they've learned.

10. Facilitate acquiring power

Inherent in the name "empowering leader" is the notion that they facilitate the accrual of power. They understand that for people to feel in control of their lives, they need to be empowered. For people to be effective in their work, they need to feel in control of their lives. They understand how to empower others, and they go out of their way to help others become more powerful and more in control.

The empowering leaders understand where both personal and organizational power come from and they are not afraid to empower others, even when those others may, in time, surpass the leader. They are not afraid to have the pupil surpass the teacher.

Conclusion

All these supervisory roles and responsibilities assume one thing in common. They assume a mature and responsible employee who is willing and able to accept the roles and responsibilities that face the front-line employee in the downsizing organization. We describe these roles and responsibilities in the following chapter.

If senior executives hope to break the fear-distrust cycle, they need to address areas that directly impact the level of trust people have in their organization.

The vision. *Most organizations have a formal vision statement of the ideal state. But do individuals "own" the vision?*

The values. *Values are beliefs or convictions that guide behavior and support the vision.*

The compensation system. *For a compensation to be perceived as fair, leaders need to follow a consistent and honest approach.*

- *Share salary ranges with associates as appropriate.*
- *Make merit pay decisions based on objective data that reflect actual performance.*
- *Make bonus systems quantifiable.*
- *Conduct internal equity comparisons for the same or similar jobs.*
- *Conduct external market equity comparisons for key jobs.*
- *Ensure that all employees share in the gains and that senior executives' pay is based on results.*

The work environment. *Working conditions affect how people perceive whether top-level managers really care about them.*

Personnel decisions. *To build trust, leaders must make decisions such as hiring, firing, appraising, promoting, and transferring based on objective data.*

Robert W. Rogers, *Executive Excellence, 7/94*

Summary Map

Manager/Supervisor Roles and Responsibilities

Uniqueness of manager/supervisor responsibilities

Managers/supervisors are in a unique position in a downsizing organization. They are employees and share the roles and responsibilities of downsized employees However, they are also leaders and share some of the downsizing reponsibilities of executives. Finally, they have responsibilities unique to their nonexecutive leadership positions.

Major responsibility during downsizing

Managers/Supervisors are responsible for helping employees make the transition from a loyalty basis to a congruence basis for employee commitment:

- Model the new basis of affiliation with the organization.
- Articulate the organizational and personal values inherent in given actions or decisions.
- Clearly identify goals or objectives for given actions or decisions.
- Articulate skills and knowledge required to achieve goals and objectives.
- Demonstrate a reasonable understanding of the transferability or desirability of those skills in the general employment market.

Additional manager/supervisor responsibilities

Provide the basis for motivation:

- Know what the task involves and what it takes to perform the task.
- Engender the feeling that the employee has a reasonable chance for success.
- Provide an understanding of the probable consequences of successfully completing the task (as well as of failing and only partially completing the task).
- Build a desire in the employee to accomplish the desired results.

Facilitate the development of skills employees will need after downsizing and realignment:

- If you cannot identify a needed, tangible outcome, don't invest in the developmental activity.
- Focus on developmental activities that provide employees with processes for developing answers to problems.
- Choose only developmental activities where you can define what successful completion of the activity will produce.
- Look for developmental opportunities in every action or decision, especially failures (we learn better from our mistakes).
- Give employees the opportunity to teach and learn from each other.

Motivate self and decide how best to become a substantive member of the new, emerging management team:

- Identify yourself with the management team.
- Rebuild truth and trust.
- Be truthful and keep promises.
- Back your employees.

Become a source of dependable, accurate, unemotional information for all employees.

The expanded workload

- There is more of the same work being done by fewer people.
- There is new and different work to do.

Managing the expanded workload

Identify who is best suited for a given task.

Empower employees:

- Look at the world differently than you did as a traditional leader.
- Know your strengths and weaknesses.
- Learn to tolerate risk taking.
- Set high standards for yourself and others.
- Share credit with others.
- Lead by example.
- Believe in people.
- Value diversity.
- Encourage sharing.
- Facilitate the acquisition of power.

Chapter 7

Employee Roles and Responsibilities

For many people downsizing is the organizational equivalent of the tornado that carried the unwilling Dorothy from Kansas to the land of Oz. It is an unpredictable and uncontrollable force that destroys everything in its path with a random and wanton disregard for the lives it touches. But unlike a tornado, downsizing is thought to be a human phenomenon and because it is supposedly under human control, there is a widely held belief that the destructive forces of downsizing must be somebody's fault.

The tornado transported Dorothy from Kansas to Oz where she came face to face with her nemesis, the Wicked Witch of the West. And the bad things that happened to Dorothy in Oz could be blamed on the Wicked Witch.

Downsizing cannot be blamed on some wicked witch. But bad things do happen to good people when an organization downsizes and those bad things must be somebody's fault. Someone has to be blamed. In our search for a nemesis, for someone to point the accusatory finger at, we have settled on a vague collective sense of the people we imagine to have been in control: the managers, the leaders, the decision makers. *They* did it. The bad is *their* fault.

Some base the blame on the Scarecrow argument: if only *they* had a brain. Downsizing is all about incompetence. *They* should have seen it coming. *They* never should have hired all these people in the first place. *They* should have anticipated the increased competition, the technological change, the deregulation of the industry. *They* should have known. After all, *they* were at the head of the organization so *they* should have been responsible for the thinking. *They* should have seen it coming.

For others, the basis for assigning the blame is the Tin Woodsman argument: if only *they* had a heart. Downsizing can be blamed on men and women who substituted personal greed for compassion. If *they* cared about us and the people like us *they* never would have chosen to downsize. *They* would have found another way to save both the organization and our jobs. *They* would have shared in the pain and taken less for themselves so that, at least in the short run, we could have had our share for a little longer.

Still others use the Cowardly Lion argument: if only *they* had courage. *They* could have made the tough decisions, told their constituents, the unions, the government, the stockholders, "No". If *they* had had the courage to do the right thing, whatever that might have been, then we wouldn't be in this mess now. *They* chose to take the easy path, to make the convenient choices, to cave in to the pressure. *They* buckled under to the internal politics, afraid to stand tough.

In the story of Oz, Dorothy just wants to get back to Kansas. She wants to go home, where everything is the way it is supposed to be. She wants to be magically transported back to her old, comfortable reality.

As victims and/or survivors or downsizing, employees also want to be transported. They dream of returning to a land where downsizing never comes, where jobs last forever and where every year they get a cost-of-living adjustment, a raise and, in the good years, a Christmas bonus.

The unfortunate message for these dreamers is that there is no Kansas. There is no Wizard. There are no ruby slippers. And worst of all, there is no one to blame. Downsizing is a reality. It occurs because change, like the tornado, is an uncontrollable and unpredictable force of nature.

They are not villains. *They* are people, most of whom were simply doing the best they could do with what they had.

But weren't *they* incompetent? Some were. And so were some of their employees, sticking to time honored practices and work rules long after they had lost their utility and letting inertia carry them along rather than seeking and embracing innovation.

But, weren't *they* greedy? Some were. And so were some of their employees, insisting on raises and job security, benefits and pensions, long after reality told them that the organization could ill afford them.

But weren't *they* cowardly, heartless, all of those things that employees desperately wish they were, so they could blame someone for their hard times? Some were. And by fixating on who to blame, rather than taking responsibility for what happens next, so are many employees.

There were no intelligent, compassionate or courageous managers in charge of Wonderland. There were only the Munchkins, witches, flying monkeys and other native inhabitants of this special world. And then there was Dorothy, a stranger in this alien and sometimes hostile environment. Like many survivors of downsizing, she began her adventure bewildered, uncertain, fearful, angry and upset. How was it then that she survived?

There were four keys to Dorothy's success:

1. **Goals**—Dorothy knew what she was trying to accomplish. She had a clear and specific set of goals: get to Emerald City, find the wizard, return to Kansas.
2. **Persistence**—Dorothy never lost sight of her long-term goals despite the many short-term distractions Oz held in store.
3. **Adaptation**—She continually changed her tactics to meet the challenges she found there, even when the outcome was uncertain.
4. **Responsibility**—Dorothy came to realize that she could not depend on anyone else to solve her problems. The wizard and the good witch tried to help in whatever ways they could, but the ultimate responsibility was hers.

Unlike the case with Dorothy, the downsizing organization is no dream. Yet, neither are the lessons of goals, persistence, adaptability and personal responsibility. The individual survivors of downsizing need to get on with the work of attaining their own unique, personal success. The keys remain:

- setting personal life goals
- persisting in the effort to attain those goals
- adapting to changing circumstances and challenges
- accepting personal responsibility for your own failures and successes

Setting personal life goals

Says Bill Lowell, founder of Business Development Directives: Downsizing has pushed some people into careers or new ventures they might not have otherwise considered. For others, being fired has given them tenacity they didn't know they had. They've been downsized, they've found new jobs and they vow never to be caught off-guard again.

Paul Holley,
The Business Journal,
Milwaukee,
2/19/94

Setting personal goals is something that we have all heard about but many of us have yet to accept as critical to our success. Failure to accept the responsibility for goal setting is another example of the Christopher Columbus syndrome: not knowing where you are going, not knowing where you are, not knowing where you have been. There are experts in the field who have written extensively on both the why and how of personal goal setting.

The constants in their advice include writing a list of goals rather than keeping the list in your head. Written goals have more substance and are more likely to be useful. Written goals serve as a constant reminder and provide a tangible basis for assessing progress.

Set both long-term and interim goals. Long-term goals serve as a flag on the horizon, a visible indicator of the general direction your life should be taking. Short-term goals provide milestones which have value both as a means of checking progress and as a cause for celebration when they are reached.

Review and revise your goals periodically. They should be reviewed to ensure that you continue to pursue goals that are important to you. They should be revised to reflect changes in both your goals and your progress. If the going is tougher than expected, smaller steps in the right direction might serve as acceptable interim goals. If the interim goals are too easily attainable, they might be spread further apart. As you attain long-term goals you should consider what new goals you want to add to your list.

They should reflect a balance in your life. Goals should address the material, physical, relational, emotional and spiritual aspects of who you are. Setting goals in just one or two of these areas can lead to your life getting out of balance where you place too much emphasis on some areas and neglect others. All of the experts seem to agree that balance is necessary.

Goals should be limited to events and outcomes that are within your control. There is no value in setting goals for others since you cannot make others achieve them. Set only goals that reflect the results or efforts that you can invest.

And they should be realistic. Given your talents, abilities, nature and circumstances what could you achieve, what goals might you realize through a combination of hard work and favorable fortune? Find a set of goals that stretch you, where the possibility of failure exists but where success can be had. Don't settle for the guaranteed result, where victory is cheapened by the ease of attainment. Nor should you strive for the impossible, where failure is a certainty. Stretch, reach, but always within possibility.

In today's changing organizational climate, career goals might need to be reevaluated. Remember that it is not a failure to recognize that reality has changed and to adjust your goals to reflect that change. If, for example, your organization has flattened, eliminated layers from the organizational hierarchy and announced a freeze on promotions, it is perfectly appropriate to revise those goals which sought advancement or promotion. But when you do revise a goal downward be certain that the new goal still represents a significant accomplishment.

Finally, goals should serve as a basis for ethical and effective decision making. Every decision can be tested by simply asking three questions. Is this decision going to move me closer to one or more of my goals? Is this decision consistent with my definition of right, fair and good? Is it ethical?

Persisting in the effort to attain those goals

Persistence is one of those attributes that we associate with successful people. There are dozens of stories of the famous and not-so-famous who persisted in the pursuit of their personal goals long after other less committed people might have given up.

One personal favorite is attributed to Thomas Edison. After failing 1900 times in his attempt to identify a suitable material for use as the filament in his incandescent light bulb, Edison was supposedly asked by a science reporter if he wasn't discouraged by 1900 straight failures. His response typifies the persistent person. He told the reporter that no, he was not discouraged because he did not look upon his experiments as failures. Edison said, "These are not failures. I have successfully identified 1900 substances that will not work."

Whether you take your inspiration from Edison, from Walt Disney who fought successive bankruptcies and mental breakdowns, or from Abraham Lincoln who failed over and over again before ever winning his first elected office, look around you. There are inspirational leaders everywhere. Find your personal hero, your personal model of persistence and use that example as a standard against which to measure your own commitment.

Hollywood has made a habit of the underdog movie, where the unlikely succeed, because it satisfies our human nature to see persistence overcome adversity. It is satisfying because we recognize the attribute of persistence as one within our reach and can see ourselves in the role of the one who struggles and wins against all odds.

Persistence is not only attainable, it is necessary. Especially in today's organizational climate it is unreasonable to expect an easy path paved with gold. The more likely road we will all take is twisting, hilly and paved with loose stones as likely to trip us up as to make our way easier. Even Dorothy's yellow brick road had its stumbling blocks.

Adapting to changing circumstances and challenges

Man's mind stretched to a new idea, never goes back to its original dimensions.

Oliver Wendell Holmes

Changing times call for change. If we are to be effective in the new roles and responsibilities that comprise our jobs we have to adapt. Adapting means learning new skills and attaining new knowledge. It means redefining the who, how, what, when and where of our jobs.

Among the greatest changes we may be called upon to make is a change in our mindset. Employees in a downsizing environment have to let go of any number of preconceptions regarding the organization and the work they perform.

Employees cannot afford to maintain an entitlement mentality. They cannot subordinate themselves to the paternalistic organization and relinquish their responsibility in exchange for a set of promises. Employees cannot rely on the organization to guarantee their future well being. There are no guarantees today. All employees at every organizational level need to take back the responsibility for their lives.

Let go of the belief that you are what you do for a living. After all, you may have to change what you do. In fact, the futurists are suggesting that people entering the workforce today will not just have multiple employers, they will have multiple careers. We see this already. We know the computer programmer who became the travel agent. We know a former aircraft engine mechanic who became a computer technician and then a landscaper, and the laid-off pilot who started a pool-cleaning company.

There is some evidence to suggest that although women in organizations have an easier time, psychologically, of redefining what they do for a living, men are successful in this task all the time. But it is not easy.

The example of how this doesn't work was presented on one of the many television talk shows several years ago. A thirty-something gentleman was bemoaning his fate. His father, recently retired, had worked all his adult life for a major auto manufacturer as an engine builder in their local truck plant. The son had followed in the father's footsteps fully expecting to retire after putting in 40 years or so. The plant closed. The company relocated truck engine fabrication to a new, modern facility in another part of the country.

This young man had the sympathy of the audience for a full 30 minutes, describing the hardships he had endured as his union benefits had run out, and with him facing a job market where not even minimum wage jobs were available. He lost their sympathies with one answer.

An audience member asked why he didn't relocate to the city where the new plant had been built, or go to another part of the country where there were numerous good paying jobs awaiting people who were not afraid to work hard. His answer captured everything that is wrong with the notion of entitlement.

"Why should I have to move? I shouldn't have to sell my house. I shouldn't have to take my kids out of school. I shouldn't have to disrupt my life. I'm a truck mechanic. Why should I change jobs? Why should I have to go back to school and learn a new trade? I studied to be a truck mechanic like my father. It's their fault. They mismanaged the plant. They lost their competitive edge. They failed me. Why should I change?"

Accepting personal responsibility for your own failures and successes

Blaming others for the uncontrollable forces in nature and the bad things they impose on our lives is not only inaccurate, it is counter-productive. Staying focused on blame distracts the individual from the more effective perspective of personal responsibility, the only certain path to success. It is true that the *theys* in our lives make decisions and take actions which affect our lives, but ultimately it is we who must deal with those realities and create our own success.

Consider this young employee's story. He had been on the job for about 10 months when his supervisor, Bob, called him into the office for a formal performance review and salary discussion. Bob's opening remark was, "Jeff, we had the group review meeting yesterday. We went over every employee's performance year to date and I have to tell you, we were really disappointed in your work.

"Most of your work has been involved with the XYZ project and the most visible aspect of what you do is the monthly progress report. In fact the main reason we hired you was so I wouldn't have to do those reports every month and so I could have time to oversee the other projects our group is responsible for.

"You have done nine of these monthly reports since coming here and all nine have been unacceptable. In fact, when you turn the reports in to me they are in such bad shape that it takes me the better part of a week, working at home, nights, just to get it ready to turn into the project committee. And because it takes so long to correct a bad report, the last seven reports have been late. The project committee is upset that the reports are always late. I'm upset that they are poorly done and that I have all this extra work to do.

"When discussing your performance the supervisors all agreed that your work is not satisfactory. As a result we voted to give you an 'Unacceptable' performance rating, to put you on probation and to not give you a pay raise this time around."

Jeff, the young employee, was rocked. He thought that he had been doing a decent job. He had bought into the myth, "No news is good news." Bob never said anything about the reports being unacceptable or late, so Jeff had just gone along thinking that everything must have been all right. After all, wasn't it Bob's responsibility to tell Jeff if Jeff was failing?

Poor Jeff. His job was in jeopardy. The raise he was expecting was not there. He and his wife and their infant daughter not only couldn't afford some of the luxuries they had been hoping for, they might not even be able to afford the basic necessities if he lost this job.

In telling Jeff's story to employees and supervisors in a workshop environment, we then ask whose fault it was that Jeff was in this situation. Most workshop participants want to blame Bob, the supervisor. After all, Bob was a weak supervisor. He didn't give Jeff the feedback he deserved. He never confronted Jeff with the fact that his reports were unacceptable or that Bob was having to redo the reports at home. Bob waited until he was required to give Jeff his annual appraisal before telling him that he needed to shape up and by then it was too late.

Consider this alternative perspective. Jeff had forfeited his personal responsibilities. After all, it was Jeff's reputation on the line. It was his income, his job security, his family's well-being that were at stake. And Jeff handed that all over to Bob, a relative stranger, saying, in effect, "Here, you be responsible for all of this. You be in charge."

In our organizational society we see this play reenacted all too often. Employees entrust the organization or its representatives with responsibilities that are rightfully theirs. They give control of their lives to their employers. And then, as we have described above, they are incensed or hurt when they do not get what they want or believe they deserve from that organization.

Jeff had an obligation to himself, his family and his employer to accept those responsibilities which were rightfully his. His job effectiveness is his responsibility. He should have gone to Bob sometime after the first month's report was handed in and before beginning to prepare the second month's report and sought the information he needed. No confrontation was called for. Just a simple inquiry. "Bob, I'm about ready to start the monthly XYZ report. Is there anything I need to do differently from last month's report?"

This would have provided Bob the opportunity to give Jeff the information he needed in a timely fashion before he did eight more unacceptable reports.

Is it Bob's responsibility to tell Jeff if he is doing a poor job? Of course it is. But Jeff has a responsibility here too. After all, it is his life that is being affected by this evaluation of his work. It would be poor counsel indeed to suggest to Jeff that he entrust any organization with his future well-being. It is his responsibility as an adult member of society to know the impact of his choices. He is responsible for his actions and the consequences of those actions.

Dependency is the belief that my safety, my self-esteem, and my freedom are in the hands of other people.

Hidden bargains are destined to disappoint and when they disappoint it is too late and the feelings run so deep that they make the relationship difficult to repair.

Patriarchy becomes a refuge for our reluctance to choose adventure and pursue our own purpose.

Peter Block,
Executive Excellence,
11/94

If Jeff gives Bob that control, then Jeff deserves what he gets. He deserves to find himself on probation, waiting to see if he can keep this job. He has earned a reputation as a marginal employee with limited potential to rise through the organizational ranks to positions of influence and prestige. That is not Bob's fault. Jeff made a poor choice when he chose to trust Bob with his future. It is no different from Jeff investing his life's savings in a company that was failing. Bob was a poor supervisor, a bad place to invest.

Employees who survive downsizing have a responsibility to take control of their lives, to accept responsibility for whatever good or bad befalls them. It is irresponsible to give over that control to the boss or the union or the company. It lacks maturity to entrust any employer or organization with your ability to provide for yourself and those dependent on you. You must assume that responsibility and jealously guard it.

Part of that responsibility is knowing what is necessary for your success. There are several questions to keep in mind:

- What are the standards against which you and your work are measured?
- What are the things you must know and do if you are to survive and succeed?
- How might you attain the skills, knowledge and information needed to be successful?
- Whose help will you need and how might you attain that help?
- How can you ensure your future employability, if not your continuing employment?

The personal responsibility is yours. You cannot, in good conscience, trust the Bobs of the world with that which rightfully belongs to you. That is the nature of personal responsibility.

Personal responsibilities

There are four particular responsibilities which, while not unique to the post-downsizing environment, are common. Ultimately, the employees of the downsized organization have to decide whether or not to move beyond anger and resistance and to accept reality. They have to understand that learning is a lifelong activity, and one which they are responsible for pursuing and fulfilling. They have to redefine what success requires and decide if they are willing to put forth the effort needed to achieve their goals. Finally, they have to decide whether or not their personal goals align with the goals and objectives of the organization.

1. Moving beyond resistance

The first of the personal responsibilities is the decision to move past denial, anger, blame and guilt, to move beyond resistance into a positive position of adaptation and effectiveness. What we may fail to realize while we are embroiled in the emotions of resisting the changes associated with downsizing is that while this is a natural reaction, it is also a choice. We choose to resist. We choose to move beyond resistance. We decide how long to indulge our anger, fear, resentment, guilt and distrust. We decide when enough is enough, when to move on, if ever.

There are four motives we might examine as we consider whether or when to let go of the anger, fear and distrust which characterize resistance. Sanford Krolick called them:

- individualism
- altruism
- pragmatism
- idealism

Individualism concerns the answer to the time-honored question, "What's in it for me?" That is a legitimate concern and an important question. Employees cannot be expected to forego the concern for their own best interests. There is also a world of difference between considering the appropriate individualistic concerns and being totally self-centered. Individualism is one of four considerations. It should not be ignored. Neither should it dominate every decision.

As you consider wherever your resistance is coming from, concern for "what's in it for me" can be an equally powerful motivator for progress as it is for resistance. The real individual benefits of letting go of resistance must be recognized. It is by letting go that the employee comes out of the past and into the present, where the potential for progress exists. Holding on to useless elements of the past, like the entitlement mentality described above, serve only to prevent future successes.

Altruism concerns the impact of our choices on others and on our relationships with those others. As you consider the decision to move beyond resistance you may wish to ask yourself who, besides yourself, is affected by that decision. In the example of Jeff, above, we referenced the impact of Jeff's choices on his wife and child. We also saw how Jeff's failures made extra work for Bob and resulted in the project committee being denied current data for several months.

It can be useful to examine our resistance and ask who is being helped and who is being hurt by this choice. Customers? Stockholders? Suppliers? Coworkers? Management?

Balance that set of considerations against who would benefit or be harmed from an end to the resistance. Typically, the altruistic motive supports letting go of the resistance if the change is either benign or benevolent.

Pragmatism concerns the bottom line, practical ramifications of your decision. If the decision is to resist, then the practical effect is that a desired change, at least a change desired by the organization, is being slowed, delayed, or disrupted. That is especially the case if change is unavoidable or irreversible.

What might be the pragmatic consequences of letting go of that resistance. If the change were supported would it be more likely to succeed? Would the practical consequences of resistance or nonresistance better serve the organization's goals and objectives?

Idealism addresses the set of values and beliefs that influence your decision making. Consider your personal values and how you define rightness, goodness and fairness. Does the change you are resisting violate these values? Does resisting have its justification in these ideals? If so, is there any way you can resist less and still maintain your personal integrity, your commitment to doing what is right, good and fair?

The typical situation is that the answers to these questions of individualistic, altruistic, pragmatic and idealistic motivations are a mixed set of plusses and minuses, pros and cons. We rarely find situations where the organizational change and its consequences are 100 percent positive or 100 percent negative when assessed against these four criteria. Neither do we find resistance to be totally on one side or the other of this evaluation.

What is suggested is that, as a decision maker (and continuing to resist or letting go of resistance is a decision), you should find an appropriate balance among these four motives. You should consider all four in every decision-making situation and should let concern for all four drive your choices.

2. Relearning how to learn

The second responsibility we will discuss concerns determining what you must learn to remain employable and developing and implementing the plan to attain that learning. It means redefining what it means to learn.

For most of today's employees the assumptions about learning were that one would attend school for a predetermined number of years and then enter the working world. From that point forward, except for "professionals" with continuing education obligations, learning would be confined to specific, job-related skills training. That would take the form of on-the-job training, coaching and some classroom programs.

Professionals were a different class of employee who had to meet continuing education requirements in order to maintain their licenses and status as members in good standing of their chosen profession.

The professional model has become one way to view the short-term future. Every employee has to recognize that ongoing learning is a way of life. Part of this is technology driven. Look at the vast numbers of employees who use personal computers in their daily work. Every one of them had to learn how to use a computer, and for those who have been in the workforce more than 10 to 12 years, that was learned after formal schooling was completed. Even if you came to the job with computer skills it seems as though every six months there is a new upgrade to the software package you are using and it's back to learning.

While overall employment trends varied greatly from province to province, one consistent theme was increased demand for more highly educated labor.

Phillip Cross,
Canadian Economic Observer,
2/93

Now much of the learning is self-initiated and self-executed. Self-study is the fastest growing segment of the educational spectrum and it appears as if that trend will continue.

The self-study model applies equally to maintaining one's employability, even as the nature of the work changes, even as we change employers. And more often than not it is self-study to meet a need identified by the learner, sought out by the learner, financed by the learner and undertaken during the learner's personal time.

What makes this an even further cry from our tradition of public education is that the learner is defining the curriculum, based on some loosely drawn sense of what skills and knowledge may be required in the future. There is no prescribed curriculum for future success. Employees must gather whatever information is available about the evolving nature of their work and plot a course towards some ill-defined learning goals, without any guarantee that these are the goals that will promise success.

What learning means today is that we first define the need, then develop the strategy for meeting that need, then execute the strategy by taking the prescribed training and learning the prescribed content. We then wait, hoping that we guessed right and that the newly acquired skills and knowledge will be what we need to ensure our continuing employability with our current employer, or with some other future employer. The responsibility is ours.

In some organizations, employees are finding support from an enlightened management which realizes that it is in their vested interests to actively support and participate in the process. They help employees to identify the skills and knowledge that will be needed in the future, and to develop or acquire and then deliver and even finance the training, work time and/or other resources, such as the use of the organization's computers, classroom space and senior staff as trainers.

In most organizations, as of this writing, it is still "every man (or woman) for him (or her) self."

3. Redefining the level of effort

The third personal responsibility we will discuss concerns redefining what it will take for you to succeed. Consider Ian, a second-year university student. This was a young man who never had to work very hard in high school. He did well enough on nearly zero effort to get into the university of his choice and even earn a small scholarship.

During year one of his university experience he had to come to grips with a new reality. Going in he knew that he was going to have to work harder than he had ever worked in school before. What he did not know was just how hard he was going to have to work or if he was capable of doing what was necessary to be successful. In several conversations with this young man during this year he defended his level of effort by pointing out that he was studying harder than he had ever studied before. The unfortunate reality was that his grades were average at best, marginal in some cases.

By the end of the year he seemed to have realized that working harder than ever before was not the criterion. Working hard enough to meet the new, higher standard was what mattered. He was being held accountable for his results, not his effort. He was going to have to put forth sufficient effort to achieve the needed results if he was to remain in school.

The parallel is true for today's employee. The standard is higher. You will have to work harder today than before. But working harder is not what counts. Delivering results that meet the higher standard is what counts. One of the employees' responsibilities concerns redefining the levels of effort necessary to be successful in the new job that demands more results, sometimes in less time and with fewer resources. We, as employees in a downsized organization, must decide if we are willing to accept the legitimacy of the new standard, and if so, if we are willing to work hard enough and smart enough to deliver.

The desire among youths to improve their knowledge and skills appears well justified. The unemployment rate for young people falls as education rises, from 29.5 per cent in December 1992 for those with less than nine years of school to 6.0 per cent for university graduates. This mirrors the general situation evident in the last two years.

Phillip Cross,
Canadian Economic Observer, 2/93

4. Aligning with the redefined organization

The question of alignment is the fourth area of personal responsibility. To what extent are you, as an employee, willing to accept the goals and objectives of the new downsized organization? This transcends the question of your willingness to work hard enough to meet the new standards. It goes to the central question of your willingness to align yourself with the long-term strategic goals and objectives, post-downsizing. Are you willing to accept your place in the new organization under the new social contract of work?

That new social contract is uncertain and evolving. We have a clearer glimpse of what it is not and what it might become than of what it is. It is not an exchange of mutual loyalties. It is not a promise that seniority will be revered, that past contributions will purchase future assurances. The old social contract of work made the promise of security in exchange for loyalty. Today's contract does not.

It might be that at some future time we will have a clearly defined replacement for that old contract. One which we advocate is that employers collaborate with their employees in ensuring that employees have the opportunity and resources to develop the skills and knowledge for their next job while performing their current job. We recommend a shared, good faith effort to raise the likelihood that each employee continues to learn and develop the skills and knowledge needed to provide for future employment.

If organizations accept their share of this responsibility, they are assured a pool of useful talent in their own organizations and among those leaving other organizations. More importantly, if individuals accept this responsibility they are assured a better set of opportunities as they move from task to task, position to position, employer to employer.

Conclusion

The message of responsibility is that we must each realize that our tasks are many and varied. In the downsized organization we are being asked to assume new, different and sometimes extraordinarily challenging responsibilities as part of the new order.

We have choices to make. We can step up to the challenge or decline. Accept the burden or abdicate. Whatever our choice, we may benefit from remembering that every responsibility that is rightfully ours, which we choose to ignore, will be left unfulfilled. We cannot reasonably expect *them*, whoever *they* are, to do for us what we should rightly do for ourselves.

The most difficult lesson in downsizing may be that we are each responsible for our own successes and failures. We have no choice but to do for ourselves or do without. No free lunches. No paternalistic organization protecting us from this harsh reality. The challenge is ours. So, too, are the rewards and the gratification that come from doing that which is ours to do.

If, after a loss, you can create a mental path from the past to the future, you will be free to be proactive in the present. The following actions will help you take practical action toward recovery from a serious loss. These steps move from the past toward an acceptable future.

- *Assume the worst.*
- *Let go of any illusions of control or magical thinking.*
- *Take time to grieve, but not more than you need.*
- *Celebrate the best of what was lost; bring it symbolically with you toward the future.*
- *Visualize a positive future; it does not need to be very specific.*
- *Revisit your values and appreciate what you still have.*

Having created a path from the past to a positive future, you are now free to be proactive and productive in the present.

- *Empower yourself to take action on your own.*
- *Use your energy for building, not blaming.*
- *Guide and use your support system.*
- *Be forgiving toward yourself and others.*
- *Make a conscious effort to learn from the experience.*
- *Don't be afraid to take time off from the serious business of rebuilding your life; relax and renew yourself.*

B. Kim Barnes, *Executive Excellence*, 4/94

Summary Map

Employee Roles and Responsibilities

A fact

Sometimes bad things happen to good people during downsizing.

A myth

"They" are to blame.

Reality

There is no one to blame.

Rules for the survivors of downsizing

Set personal life goals:

- You have to know where you are going in order to know when you have arrived.
- Make a written list of goals rather than trying to keep them in your head.
- Set interim as well as long-term goals.
- Review and revise goals periodically.
- Choose goals that bring balance to your life.
- Limit goals to events and outcomes that are within your control.
- Set goals that are realistic.
- Periodically reevaluate career goals (after all it is a changing climate).
- Use goals as a basis for ethical and effective decision making.

Expend effort to attain those goals:

- Choose a personal model of persistance as a standard against which to measure your own commitment.
- Prepare yourself mentally for the struggle—you will encounter many roadblocks before you reach your destination.

Adapt to changing circumstances and challenges:

- Avoid an entitlement mentality; the organization cannot guarantee your future.
- Take personal responsibility for your life.
- Let go of the belief that you are what you do for a living.

Accept personal responsibility for your own failures and successes:

- Staying focused on blame distracts you from the desired path of accepting personal responsibility which will lead to success.
- Don't accept the myth that "no news is good news"; it is your obligation to make sure you are doing well on the job.
- Know the standards against which you and your work are measured.
- Find out what you must know and do in order to succeed.
- Determine how to attain the skills and knowledge needed for success.
- Whose help will you need to succeed and how will you obtain that help?
- How can you maintain your future employability, if not your continuing employment?

Responsibilities in the post-downsizing environment

- Move beyond resistance to change.
- Relearn how to learn.
- Redefine the level of effort it will take to succeed when faced with new standards.
- Align yourself with the redefined organization.

Chapter 8

The Silver Lining

We conclude this book with a shift from the pragmatic to the philosophical. In this chapter we look at some real and potential benefits, if not from the downsizing itself, then from the forces which bring it about. Our focus in this chapter is on large-scale change, not individual fortune.

That is not to say that there have not been countless individuals who now claim that being ousted via downsizing was the "best thing that ever happened to me." Many successful entrepreneurs give credit to the downsizing, and the separation allowance or cash incentives it brought, for their finally finding their niche in life. Schools are filled with former employees who have used the opportunity afforded by the loss of their job to seek a more fulfilling life doing work that they hope will add more meaning and joy to their future years.

But for every person looking fondly back on the good fortune following the downsizing of their former employer, there are several who are without work or stuck in lower paying jobs. There are those who have a lower standard of living. They may not be the big cities' homeless and forgotten. But they are the overeducated cab drivers and laborers whose education no longer matches the needs of the organizational community. They are the modern John Henrys, unskilled laborers whose jobs are now being done more cheaply and more efficiently by some technological innovation with which they could not compete. They are the semi-skilled who saw their jobs exported to another region of the world where contemporary technology and/or cheap labor conspired to make them noncompetitive. They are the victims who will never accept that they are better off for the downsizing, because in their lives that is not true.

Nor do we wish to ignore the reality that numerous organizations have not only survived, but prospered when they employed downsizing as an integral element of their success strategy.

Rather, we wish to refocus on the global perspective, since it is that broadest view which provides a context for understanding the overall systemic value of downsizing.

Fundamental change

The long-term effects of downsizing aren't as clear cut. Observers see positives and negatives for the economy.

Paul Holley, *The Business Journal*, Milwaukee, 2/19/94

The fundamental nature of organizations is evolving, and global downsizing is a symptom of that evolution. But this is not something new. In the period ranging from the 1920s through the 1950s organizations were built on principles derived from the assembly line and the military.

The military contributed structures which applied the concept of the chain of command to organizational hierarchies. Reporting relationships were formalized and sequential. The immediate superior became the focal individual for the front-line employee.

The assembly line contributed the narrowing of the job's scope and the idea of interchangability. People who performed like tasks lost their individuality. They became as interchangeable as the machines that performed the less complex tasks.

Performance was measured in group or unit output. Individuals were tasked to keep up with the line. Individual improvements in performance flowed from efficiencies in how the task was structured, and were dictated by the process consultants of the day, the efficiency experts, armed with stopwatch and clipboard as they performed time and motion studies.

Given the state of the global economy and the state of our understanding of the nature of organizations, these structures and concepts fit the times.

Those of us who entered the workforce in the 1950s and 1960s came into a system of organizations that was evolving. We saw the first attempts by professors of management to rehumanize work. We encountered theories of management and leadership which suggested that more attention to the human side of management would complement the focus on task and technology, resulting in a healthier, more effective organization.

The time and motion study gave way to attitude surveys, style inventories and needs analyses. The process consultant of the day focused on communications, information flow and the locus of decision-making authority. Management by objectives displaced time and motion as the measures of effectiveness. Work was being rehumanized.

Today's reengineering is a balanced approach to organizational effectiveness which considers all aspects of the organization as we currently understand it. Nadler's OPM (Organization Performance Model) is the archetype. It is strategic, systemic and comprehensive, integrating everything we believe we understand about how organizations function. For the first time we are operating from a paradigm that is equally focused on external forces affecting the organization as it is on the internal structures and performers.

Given this shift in our understanding of the fundamental nature of organizations, downsizing is not only understandable, but both inevitable and appropriate. Downsizing has its positive side.

The positive aspects of downsizing

It is difficult to discuss the positive aspects of the downsizing phenomenon because of all the pain experienced by those whose individuality is masked by the statistics and generalizations. There is no denying that downsizing at its best disrupts and at its worst destroys. There are countless newspaper accounts of families torn apart by the after effects of one or more members being victimized by the strategic blade cutting both fat and lean from the organizational body.

Some are true victims, the unwitting and undeserving, whose lives are forever changed because the organizational decision makers incorrectly saw downsizing as the right answer to some poorly formed question of cost savings or competitive advantage. They are victims in the sense that, for their situation, downsizing was the wrong choice, poorly implemented. Their sacrifice was for naught, as the promises of prosperity and future success were drowned in a sea of mismanagement and ineptitude. It is small consolation for these victims that the same incompetent management that laid them off would have quickly led the organization to its inevitable failure by some other path had they not downsized.

But organizational failures and the uprooting of employees' lives is neither new nor is it unique to the decision to downsize. It is the natural consequence of what some call organizational Darwinism, survival of the fittest. This position asserts that the competitive jungle of business and government is not unlike the competitive jungle in which beasts struggle daily to eat without being eaten. Simply put, not every organization can survive. Those that do are the ones which demonstrate their fitness and their ability to do what the laws of the jungle demand. And as we will see, downsizing is an organizational fitness strategy.

Darwinism

Darwin's argument was not always easy to follow, and over the years the idea of survival of the fittest has been misquoted too often. In the natural order of the world according to Darwin, fitness was not an individual trait. It was the survival of a species, not the individual, that was at issue. That form of survival was measured by the species' success at reproduction, and the survival of one generation of offspring to sexual maturity and the reproduction of the next generation. Being eaten by a natural predator after completing the reproductive obligation to the species did not affect overall fitness. By that stage of development and maturity the individual had fulfilled its purpose, and its continuing existence was no longer critical to fitness, and thus to survival.

Continuing the example, if two individuals combined to produce two offspring, both of whom survived to reproduce, then those two individuals had replaced themselves in the overall population of that particular species and thus contributed to its survival. If a breeding pair produced one thousand offspring, of which 998 died or were killed prior to reproduction of the following generation, that pair was equally successful. Darwin was not looking at individual strength or longevity when discussing survival of the fittest.

Likewise the argument for natural selection, what we call evolution, is also bound up in the definition of survival as the ability to reproduce offspring who survive to reproduce offspring of their own. A genetic or behavioral characteristic or trait appears in an individual which increases the ability of that individual to reproduce successful offspring. When that trait or characteristic is passed along, the "fitness" of those who possess or demonstrate that trait is increased. Nature "selects" those whose survivability is thus enhanced. They and their offspring survive in greater proportion than those who lack the trait. Over time the character of the species evolves so that the trait in question is common.

Organizational Darwinism

Given this view of survival and evolution we can build a construct that we can call Organizational Darwinism. This model of organizational fitness does not require the survival of every individual organization or of every employee. Neither does it require the survival of any organization beyond its fertile years. Fitness requires the generation of offspring who reach reproductive maturity. Organizations are born, grow, reproduce and die in this scenario. Those that fail to grow and reproduce do not contribute to the survival of the species. When a characteristic emerges that enhances an organization's survivability, and that trait is passed along to others, it may, over time, emerge as a critical survival characteristic.

Taking the argument to its logical conclusion, if we can show that downsizing is an adaptive trait which leads to increasing the survivability of individual organizations and of organizations in general, then we have a macro-level argument that suggests that downsizing may serve a purpose larger than the economic salvation of a given entity.

Downsizing may be an adaptation to changes in the environment which increases the survivability of those organizations which can adapt by including downsizing in the repertoire of management choices, applying that choice when called for, and resisting the temptation to downsize when it is not called for.

Organizational growth and reproduction

We all understand organizational growth intuitively. More employees, more customers, more product and more revenue all signal growth. But what is organizational reproduction?

Typically it is the natural consequence of an organization successfully identifying and/or creating a need and then serving it in such a way that its success attracts competitors. Whether in the private or public sectors, manufacturing or service, for profit or nonprofit, fit organizations create and attract competitors as their form of reproduction. From that expanded pool of players in the defined market, only the most capable survive. The weak players fail, the strong survive.

Consider these examples of organizations which attracted and/or created competitors. AT&T created MCI and Sprint by first creating a worldwide dependence on the ability to reach out and touch each other. Technology, political agendas and the insistence of a start-up competitor then drove the decision to deregulate long distance telephony. Had telephony never been the success it was, had long distance telecommunications not become so critical a capacity, MCI, Sprint or any of the other long distance competitors would have stayed away from this particular market in droves. In this case the original organization and some of the competitors continue to thrive. Some of the competitors have fallen by the wayside.

We can argue that IBM created Apple, which in turn recreated IBM. Computing was becoming essential as a business tool. The management of mass quantities of data was proving necessary as management became more complex. Apple's peculiar adaptation was to create a need for personal computing by creating the capacity to perform personal computing. Apple's success changed the way the market viewed the computer and in turn how IBM viewed the market. The new, reinvented (evolved?) IBM created the IBM-PC. Again, IBM, Apple and several others continue to profit in this market. Others have come and gone.

Similarly, GM invented Toyota which in turn reinvented GM. General Motors and the rest of the United States' "Big Three" ignored market opportunities, leaving needs unmet and creating competitive opportunities for those companies responsive enough to fill the void, thereby creating the international giants, Toyota, Nissan and Honda. These were successful domestic manufacturers who evolved into international successes in large part because the U.S. auto makers were failing to adapt and reinvent themselves to meet changing demands. The success of the Japanese car makers forced Ford, Chrysler and GM to evolve. And the cycle continued. All the major Japanese players are now selling large luxury cars in addition to the small economy cars they introduced to leverage their way into the U.S. market. So they too continue to grow and change. At this writing the automotive market is healthy, international, very competitive and still evolving.

And governments are not exempt from the processes of organizational Darwinism. What is the current "reinventing government" initiative but an attempt to adapt the organization so that it can continue to grow and spawn offspring that can perpetuate the species?

Government ineptitude, real or perceived, has led to the continuing privatization of any number of functions. Private organizations are encroaching on former natural government monopolies in education, corrections and waste management. Even the government's exclusive right to delivery of the mail, which dates back to the Articles of Confederation, is being challenged. Organizations like Federal Express and UPS are taking letter and package traffic away from the postal services of the U.S. and nearly every foreign country. And businesses, mistrusting the post offices' reliability and speed, are increasingly relying on faxes and modems to transmit what formerly they would mail.

The bright side: downsized, efficient companies become better competitors in world markets, said Steven Crane, a Marquette University economics professor.

Paul Holley,
The Business Journal,
Milwaukee,
2/19/94

In this example, at least in the U.S., the Postal Service is still fighting to define its niche and to win back the trust of its former customers. Services like Express Mail and Priority Mail, as well as the natural monopoly afforded by bulk (junk) mail, are redefining that niche.

As the above suggests, organizations spawn competitors in two ways. Success attracts competition. If your organization can thrive in a given niche, perhaps there is room in there for one or two more. This attraction is most evident when the market demand outpaces the incumbent organization's capacity to deliver.

Success also attracts when the initial need is met at a high price and the potential competitor, having been saved the cost of creating the initial demand, sees a way to meet some of the need for a lower price or with low cost enhancements.

Failure also attracts, as we have seen above. Customer dissatisfaction can be an equally tempting motive for competitors to enter the fray, if they believe that they can win customers away from the incumbent organization by providing more value while meeting the need.

All of this is fairly fundamental to our understanding of competition. How does it relate to downsizing?

Darwinian downsizing

If downsizing is a competitive adaptation and if competitive adaptations help organizations mature and spawn even more robust offspring, then downsizing may be a contributor to the general health of organizations as a species. Even in the example above we see both the primary organization and its emerging competitors using downsizing as a strategic tool for meeting the ever increasing demands for efficiency, quality, service and responsiveness fostered by the leapfrogging rise in customer expectations which results from each competitor vying to out do the others in order to increase or maintain market share.

Most of the organizations named above have downsized in order to increase their competitiveness. And they have done so successfully. They are doing better now than many detractors had forecast. They continue to employ thousands and serve millions. They are smaller than before, but in their success they have not only spawned competitors, increasing the total population of those who serve the market with that particular product or service, but they have produced support companies, suppliers, distributors and others by the hundreds.

The nature of the benefit

As we stated above, it is difficult to discuss the positive aspects of downsizing because of all the individual pain it brings. People in pain have a hard time remaining objective and detached. While their heads can understand the logic of the decision, their hearts ache with the human suffering the decision brings. That is true for both the decision makers and those who are even more directly affected.

Yet one reality is that there are positive consequences of this difficult choice. We will focus on three:

- increased competitiveness
- educational pressures
- global focus

1. Increased competitiveness

Downsizing, when all is said and done, is a response to competition for customers. Levitt said that organizations exist to attract and retain customers. Downsizing is about making the organization fitter as it pursues that goal.

Whether we are the stockholder and customer of the downsizing corporation or the voter and taxpayer of the downsizing government, the downsizing itself serves the organization by making it more likely that it can attract and/or retain us as its customer. It allows for lower costs, and therefore lower prices and higher profits in the private sector. It drives down the cost of governing and helps control or moderate taxes in the public sector.

This element of downsizing is perhaps the most discussed and best understood potential benefit. The caution needs restating, however. This is a potential benefit, not an assured benefit. As we have detailed in the preceding chapters all the strategic considerations; implementation and employee; supervisor and executive issues, roles and responsibilities must be properly managed if this promise is to be realized.

2. Educational pressures

External to the organization and one dominant, yet indirect result of the pattern of global downsizing, is the pressure on the world's educational systems. People are being pressured to attain more education. Educational institutions are being pressured to make their offerings more flexible, focused and usable if they are to continue to attract and retain their customers.

To some extent we can point to the employer as an historical influence which has shaped and directed the amounts and types of education young people sought and which institutions provided.

In our agrarian past, before universal education, home schooling in the arts and sciences of our future vocations was sufficient. The young person growing up learned those things necessary to continue the work of his or her parent. Boys learned men's work. Girls learned women's work. If the parent's work was not to be the child's work the child was apprenticed to a master of whatever work was to become that child's future.

Employment rose only for those with at least high school graduation or more education, whereas it fell sharply for those with less than a high school education. This reinforces the point that education, not experience, increasingly determines one's ability to compete and succeed in today's labour market.

Phillip Cross,
Canadian Economic Observer,
2/93

As we became industrialized, the employer continued to provide the specific education and training needed to do the work even when employees came out of the public system of universal education with the basic three R's. As work became more specialized, so did the pressures of future employers on the individual learner and the educational system.

In the 1950s employers in the U.S., facing up to political pressures, sent out a call for more engineers. There was going to be work in defense and aerospace. America needed to catch up with Russia. The Cold War and Sputnik created the work. Employers recruited those with the appropriate education. And they became those on the fast track to the pot of gold at the end of the rainbow we called the American Dream. Any high schooler who had an aptitude for math or science was directed to the engineering field by well-intentioned guidance counselors. Universities expanded their engineering departments, actively competing to attract the best and brightest engineering students.

In the 1980s the golden path was a business degree.

In the 1990s we are less certain what path leads to the realization of the dream. The futurists are telling today's young people that they will change careers during their lifetimes. Perhaps a generalist's education, including a sizable dose of humanities and social sciences is the right preparation. But no matter what you learn, it will not be enough. Be prepared for a lifetime of learning. Even employers have taken up the cry and are recruiting today's best and brightest with promises of lifetime learning and learning organizations.

Downsizing brings a new set of educational pressure. Better educated people are encountering more opportunities in an expanding world labor market. Those with the fewest skills or the most rudimentary skills are bearing the brunt of the pressure to find jobs in a diminishing job market. But education is not enough. It has to be the right education, and what constitutes "right" keeps changing.

One young woman we know is, at age 24, fluent in English, Japanese and Chinese languages. She has lived extensively in both Eastern and Western cultures, attended American, Chinese and Japanese universities. She understands the traditions and customs of these varied cultures. This is a young woman who can "write her own ticket" or so she has been told by numerous potential employers. Add a little marketing or business to her curriculum vitae and she can pick and choose among the offers from the sales and marketing departments of many international giants. Add some politics or international relations to the mix and she can find a place anywhere from the visitors and convention bureaus of the larger cities to any number of embassies or consulates to the State Department or Ministry. What she has is right for today's job market.

The same is true for her younger brother. His interests are less academic. His passion is mechanical, not cultural. He loves cars. As a university student he is creating a "mix and match" curriculum, combining business education from his hometown university with automotive repair from the local technical institute. His dream is to manage an automotive franchise. He needs business, sales, finance and mechanical expertise to realize his dream. The key to his future is a hybrid education that no school he knows is prepared to offer. His insight into the education needed for success will serve him well.

Both of these young people represent some of the best of what downsizing is helping to create. They are anticipating what the governments that run our schools need to attend to. Downsizing and the changing nature of business and government is reshaping the skill and knowledge set needed for success. The curricula of public and private schools need to realign. So do our beliefs that education is finite and for the young. So do our beliefs that one education is sufficient for a lifetime because we will each have only one career in our lifetime.

The learning individual, like the learning organization, will be the hallmark of this era in the evolution of organizations and their employees.

3. Global focus

Perhaps the greatest benefit associated with the forces surrounding downsizing is one which touches all humanity. Global competition is often cited as the villain. It is that competition which forces modernization, lower wages and the closing of inefficient or ineffective plants and factories. It is that very competition which has driven the complacent organizational giants of the sixties and seventies to become the "lean and mean" competitors of the eighties and nineties.

Although it is a bloodless competition, it is fought hard, and there are real casualties. It, like any war, is fought and won by the sweat and sacrifice of the many, who did not create the conflict. And like all wars there are innocent victims and needless, wasteful tragedies.

But unlike conventional war, global competition holds out a promise of peace. Downsizing is a strategic decision aimed at helping any given organization survive in these times of intense, often global, competition to attract and retain its customers. There will be victims, and their pain will be real. But as the evolution continues, as the future employees are better educated to succeed in this competitive arena, perhaps there will be a corollary increase in the interdependency and interconnectedness of governments and businesses throughout the world. Perhaps the walls between historically opposed nations and cultures will be "downsized" as well.

International pacts such as NAFTA (the North American Free Trade Agreement) and GATT (the General Agreement on Tariffs and Trade) are blamed for incenting organizations to relocate, seek cheaper wages, close inefficient plants and export jobs. They are derided for forfeiting national sovereignty in favor of freer world trade. Yet, they may also serve as a deterrent to the bloodier types of global conflict. Trade wars are fought with dollars, francs, pounds and yen, not nuclear-tipped missiles.

The lessons learned during the oil embargoes of the 1970s were a very powerful example of financial interdependence as a moderator of hostilities. Once the oil cartels owned significant pieces of the foreign nations dependent on their oil, it became in their vested interests that the economy of those nations be maintained. A strong U.S. economy, for example, was important to the OPEC nations because the U.S. represented a sizable customer base and because of the vastness of Arab property and business holdings in the U.S.. Driving the U.S. economy to its knees would eliminate a valued customer and would result in huge losses as business and property values held by the Arabs plummeted.

Perhaps the greatest benefit humanity will derive from the very forces which pressure organizations to downsize will be a redefinition of the arena for human conflict.

Conclusion

Not to minimize the individual pain experienced by all of downsizing's victims, but there is a greater good that is emerging.

At the macro level we see a maturing of the competitors. Like professional sports leagues and franchises there is an emerging parity. Competing organizations are finding the quality of play and of players is spiraling upward. The resulting efficiency and product and service quality benefits all the stakeholders in the enterprise, whether it be manufacturing, government, education, services, the media, the professions or the arts. Better, faster and cheaper is not just a goal. It is becoming a reality and will be a driver for continuous improvements in the foreseeable future.

Concurrent with the increased effectiveness of organizations, we are seeing a resurgence in interest in their ethics. It is not enough to compete effectively. One must compete ethically. Free trade presumes a "level playing field" and that precludes any nation or industry from relying on unethical practices to gain a competitive edge. While there is still a long way to go, and the path is filled with potential missteps and backsliding, there is a gradual progress towards a time when ethics and social responsibility will be part of how we all define success.

At the micro level there is an increasing awareness that organizations are more than a collection of interchangeable machines and machine parts. They are human creations that are of and for people. In the face of accelerating automation and mechanization we are witnesses to a renewal in the understanding of the essential nature of humanity. Organizations are about people—people who are free to make decisions and accept responsibility for those decisions; people who seek connectedness with others, social acceptance and self-actualization.

We serve each other through the instrumentality called organizations, but if we are to be well served or of service to others we must first preserve the essentials which make us truly human. The rehumanization of the organizations which we have created to serve us better will be founded on truth and trust: the essence of humanity.

In the new world of work, each person has more responsibility and more autonomy with less job security and less supervision. We can no longer hide out in the endless corridors of mammoth corporations. These giants have had an obesity problem that is being attacked with ferocity and commitment that only the fear of survival itself can generate. But as they shed excess weight, obsolete processes, redundant procedures, and bloated staffs, we witness new vitality, energy, and creativity. Andrew Grove, CEO of Intel, notes: "A corporation is a living organism, and it has to continue to shed its skin. Methods have to change. Focus has to change. Values have to change. The sum total of those changes is transformation."

David McNally, *Executive Excellence*, 3/94

Information Map

The Silver Lining

Organizations from the 1920s to the 1950s

Organizations built on principles adapted from the military and from the assembly–line experience:

- Military contributed the concept of chain of command which produced organizational hierarchies.
- Assembly line contributed the narrowing of the job's scope and the idea of interchangability.

Performance was measured in group or unit output.

Organizations from the 1950s to present day

- Organizations are rehumanizing work.
- Organizational effectiveness is now considered to include all aspects of work: strategic, systemic and comprehensive.
- Operating from a paradigm that is equally focused on external as well as internal forces
- Strict chain of command replaced with empowered teams
- Job scope expanded
- More objective measurement systems put in place

Negative aspects of downsizing

- At its best downsizing disrupts; at its worst, it destroys.
- There are some true victims of downsizing who suffer when inappropriate decisions are made.

Positive aspects of downsizing

- Increased competitiveness results as the organization makes itself fitter to participate in the marketplace.
- Downsizing produces pressure for lifetime education which produces a more capable workforce.
- Downsizing is a strategic decision aimed at helping any given organization survive global competition.

Appendix A

Pre–Downsizing Analysis

The following 45 questions are based on David Nadler's Organization Performance Model (OPM). According to this model, organizations are systems. Before making any significant strategic change, such as the decision to downsize, it is useful to systematically review the motives behind the change and the impact of the decisions and actions needed to ensure the change's success.

This series of questions can help clarify whether or not downsizing is the right response to the external and internal forces for change. There is neither a score from this review nor a passing or failing grade. It is a nonquantifiable analysis, requiring the questioner to weigh the various factors in order to reach a conclusion.

The questions listed below suggest a line of inquiry. They are not representative of a complete or detailed examination of the issue, merely a beginning of the consideration the decision to downsize warrants. Yet, unfortunately, even this limited series of questions is more extensive than those typically used to make the downsizing decision.

While these questions are couched in terms appropriate for a review of downsizing as an organizational response, the questions can be easily reformatted to allow a similar pattern of systemic inquiry for any strategic consideration.

Environment

1. What is happening outside the organization to suggest that the organization would benefit from the decision to downsize?
2. Which institutions, groups and individuals are likely to be positively affected by the proposed downsizing?
3. Which institutions, groups and individuals are likely to be negatively affected by the proposed downsizing?

Resources

4. What tangible resources will be conserved if the decision to downsize is implemented?

5. What tangible resources will need to be invested if the decision to downsize is implemented?

6. What will be the impact of this decision on intangible resources such as the organization's reputation with key stakeholders?

History

7. What patterns of effective past behavior will be maintainable during and after the downsizing?

8. What patterns of effective past behavior will not be maintainable during and after the downsizing?

9. Which recent key decisions and/or organizational commitments will downsizing support or undermine?

Mission

10. In what ways will downsizing help this organization better fulfill its stated purpose?

11. In what ways will downsizing allow this organization to better serve its customers?

12. What competitive advantages will downsizing give this organization?

Vision and values

13. In what ways will downsizing help move this organization closer to the attainment of its ultimate vision?

14. Which of this organization's values support the decision to downsize?

15. Which of this organization's values do not support the decision to downsize?

Strategic goals and objectives

16. Which current strategic goals and objectives can be better met by a downsized organization?
17. Which new strategic goals and objectives can be better met by a downsized organization?
18. Which current strategic goals and objectives cannot be met if the organization decides to downsize?

Strategic plans

19. How must this organization's resources be reallocated if it is to meet its strategic goals and objectives with fewer people?
20. What existing strategic initiatives must be maintained despite the decision to downsize?
21. What existing strategic initiatives must be sacrificed if the decision is made to downsize?

Work

22. How will the basic work of the organization be different if the downsizing decision is implemented?
23. What new skills and knowledge will workers need to be effective in the downsized organization?
24. In what ways will the work of the downsized organization be either more or less gratifying to employees?

Individuals

25. To what extent are current employees suited to the emerging downsized organization?
26. What needs/requirements do your employees have which will be easy/difficult to satisfy post-downsizing?
27. In what ways will the downsized organization motivate and reward employees?

Formal organizational arrangements

28. How will formal structures such as reporting relationships, job designs, methods and practices differ after downsizing?
29. What standards and measurements will take on increased importance in the downsized organization?
30. How will your human resources be managed differently, including evaluations and rewards, after the downsizing?

Informal arrangements

31. What existing norms and understandings will no longer be applicable/supported in the downsized organization?
32. How must supervisors and managers behave differently in an environment where more is expected from fewer people?
33. What will be the impact of downsizing on the interpersonal arrangements that support work as it is done today?

Organizational outputs

34. In what ways will downsizing affect the organization's ability to adapt to continuing changes in its environment?
35. In what ways will downsizing affect the organization's ability to allocate resources to meet changing requirements?
36. How will downsizing change the specific measurable goals, such as financial performance, that this organization seeks to attain?

Group/unit outputs

37. In what ways will downsizing increase the ability of individual groups and units to achieve their desired productivity levels?
38. In what ways will downsizing increase the ability of individual groups and units to achieve their desired quality levels?
39. In what ways will downsizing increase the ability of individual groups and units to cooperate/collaborate with each other?

Individual outputs

40. What will be the impact of this change on individual employees' ability to perform the tasks at hand?
41. What will be the impact of downsizing on individual employees' motivation and morale?
42. What will be the impact of this change on individual employees' work habits?

Feedback

43. What mechanisms will exist to help the downsized organization learn from its ability or failure to attain its goals?
44. What mechanisms will exist to help the downsized organization monitor the effectiveness of how it does its work?
45. How will this organization keep track of changes, both internal and external, which might affect its ability to succeed?

Appendix B

Downsizing Effectiveness Checklist

The 72 statements in this checklist describe the ideal situation following a downsizing. To use this checklist, simply ask to what degree each of your employees would agree that each of these statements is true in your organization, now that you have downsized.

[These questions are available formatted as an employee survey. To receive a preview copy of the *Downsizing Effectiveness Questionnaire* contact Navran Associates, Atlanta, Georgia, USA. (404) 493-8886.]

Deciding to downsize

1. Employees understand why management felt it was necessary to downsize.
2. People agree that downsizing was necessary and appropriate for this organization.
3. People from all levels of the organization participated in making the decision.
4. The decision was well thought out, not a knee-jerk reaction to short-term pressures.
5. Alternatives to downsizing were considered to achieve the desired outcomes.
6. The long-term effects of this decision are well understood.

Implementing the decision to downsize

7. Employees were given sufficient notice that downsizing was being considered.
8. People were kept posted on the progress of the decision-making process.
9. Criteria for selecting who would leave were well understood.

10. Criteria for selecting who would leave were fair and appropriate.
11. Decisions on who would leave considered individual circumstances and needs.
12. Announcements of who would be leaving were handled with dignity and respect.

Caring for those who had to leave

13. People who had to leave were given some flexibility in timing their departure.
14. People were given the option of relocating within the organization, where feasible.
15. People who had to leave had ample time to plan for their departure.
16. The organization offered optional interim benefits for those who had to leave.
17. People who had to leave were given training to help them find new positions.
18. The financial support given to those who had to leave was fair and equitable.

Impact of downsizing on customers

19. Customer service quality is as good now as it was before downsizing.
20. Customers find it just as easy to reach an employee now as before downsizing.
21. Customers know who to contact if they need assistance.
22. Customer calls are answered as quickly now as before downsizing.
23. The quality of technical assistance is as good now as before downsizing.
24. Customer complaints are taken as seriously now as before downsizing.

Impact of downsizing on quality

25. There are sufficient people to do the job right.
26. People are given sufficient time to do the job right.
27. Employees have sufficient resources and support to do the job right.
28. Continuous quality improvement is a priority.
29. We measure/monitor our work sufficiently to ensure high quality.
30. High quality is recognized/rewarded.

Trust issues after downsizing

31. Management communication with employees is honest and above board.
32. Management people routinely keep the promises they make.
33. Employees are provided with accurate and reliable information.
34. Information is provided to employees in a timely manner.
35. Employees at all levels are held to the same standards of accountability.
36. Management models the organization's values in their daily actions and decisions.

Motivation after downsizing

37. Employees have adequate opportunity for personal growth/development.
38. There is reasonable opportunity for promotion/advancement.
39. People receive appropriate recognition for excellence in their work.
40. Employees are given the opportunity to accept additional responsibility.
41. The work we perform is meaningful and fulfilling.
42. People are valued for their creativity and ideas.

Knowing what Is expected and required

43. Employees understand the organization's goals and objectives.
44. People agree with the organization's goals and objectives.
45. We know specifically what is expected/required in the performance of our jobs.
46. People understand the organization's priorities.
47. Employees understand how their jobs fit into the organization's "big picture".
48. We understand how our work contributes to the success of other employees.

Preparing for the present

49. Employees are provided with the training needed to perform their jobs.
50. People have access to the information they need to perform their jobs.
51. Current jobs are defined in clear and accurate written job descriptions.
52. Employees have the tools and technology needed to perform their jobs.
53. Training is provided that addresses both technical skills and self-development.
54. Employees are provided with sufficient budget to do the job.

Supervisory effectiveness

55. My supervisor can perform the most difficult aspects of the work he/she oversees.
56. My supervisor regularly lets us know how well we are performing our jobs.
57. If someone makes a mistake, my supervisor views that as a learning opportunity.
58. My supervisor effectively balances praise and criticism.

59. My supervisor listens to employee ideas and suggestions with an open mind.

60. My supervisor is fair in how he/she treats his/her employees.

Working relationships

61. Employees participate in making decisions that affect their jobs.

62. Cooperation and collaboration are valued in this organization.

63. Employees are rewarded for the support and assistance they provide each other.

64. My peers (others doing the same job I do) are competent and deserving of my support.

65. People I work with in other groups/units are competent and deserving of my support.

66. On balance, the help/support employees provide each other is fair and equitable.

Preparing for the future

67. The organization expects my job to change significantly in the next three to five years.

68. I know what skills and abilities will be required in this job three to five years from now.

69. Given appropriate training, I will be able to perform this job as it continues to change.

70. This organization will provide whatever training I need to do this job in the future.

71. I am developing skills here that are valued by other organizations as well.

72. My experience in this organization is good preparation for the future.

References

Atkins, Stuart. *The Name of Your Game.* Beverly Hills: Ellis & Stewart Publishers, 1981.

Blanchard, Kenneth, Ph.D. Patricia Zigarmi, Ed.D. and Drea Zigarmi, Ed.D., *Leadership and the One Minute Manager.* New York: William Morrow and Company Inc., 1985.

Block, Peter. *The Empowered Manager.* San Francisco: Jossey-Bass, 1987.

Block, Peter. *Flawless Consulting.* San Diego: Learning Concepts, 1981.

Herzberg, Frederick, Bernard Mausner and Barbara Bloch Snyderman. *The Motivation To Work.* New York: John Wiley and Sons, 1959.

Krolick, Sanford, Ph.D. *Ethical Decision-Making Style Survey and Interpretative Notes.* Beverly, Massachusetts: Addison-Wesley Training Systems, 1987.

Kübler–Ross, Elisabeth. *On Death and Dying.* New York: MacMillian, 1968.

Levitt, Theodore. *The Marketing Imagination.* New York: The Free Press, 1983.

Myers, Gail E. and Michele Tolela Myers. *The Dynamics of Human Communication: A Labortory Approach.* United States of America: McGraw-Hill, Inc., 1992.

Nadler, David A., Michael L. Tushman and Nina G. Hatvany. *Managing Organizations.* Boston: Little, Brown & Company, 1982.

Naisbitt, John. *Megatrends.* New York: Warner Books, 1984.

von Oech, Roger, Ph.D., *A Whack on the Side of the Head.* New York: Warner Books, 1983.

Peters, Thomas J. and Robert H. Waterman, Jr. *In Search of Excellence.* New York: Harper & Row, 1982.

Rodgers, Buck, with Robert Shook. *The IBM Way*. New York: Harper & Row, 1986.

Senge, Peter M. *The Fifth Discipline*. New York: Doubleday/Currency, 1990.

Executive Excellence. Provo, Utah: Executive Excellence Publishing.

Index

Notes

Notes

Notes

Notes